T0115103

PRAYING
THROUGH A
STORM

PRAYING
THROUGH A
STORM

How prayer works
How to make it work for you

THE 2ND EDITION

SHEILA GAUTREAUX

authorHOUSE®

AuthorHouse™
1663 Liberty Drive
Bloomington, IN 47403
www.authorhouse.com
Phone: 1-800-839-8640

© 2013 by Sheila Gautreaux. All rights reserved.

No part of this book may be reproduced, stored in a retrieval system, or transmitted by any means without the written permission of the author.

Published by AuthorHouse   02/18/2013

ISBN: 978-1-4817-1531-7 (sc)
ISBN: 978-1-4817-1532-4 (e)

Library of Congress Control Number: 2013903126

Any people depicted in stock imagery provided by Thinkstock are models, and such images are being used for illustrative purposes only.
Certain stock imagery © Thinkstock.

This book is printed on acid-free paper.

Because of the dynamic nature of the Internet, any web addresses or links contained in this book may have changed since publication and may no longer be valid. The views expressed in this work are solely those of the author and do not necessarily reflect the views of the publisher, and the publisher hereby disclaims any responsibility for them.

Dedication

To all of you who shared with me how much comfort you found in the first edition of this book and to all of you who return again or encounter it for the very first time.

To my Children and Grandchildren: Shawn, Stephen, Sian, Kephen, Mamadou and Shelby. To my daughter-in-law, Kristin.

Mother, thank you. I am who I am because of you and your vigilant prayers.

What readers have said . . .

"Beautifully and soulfully written, "Praying Through A Storm" is a practical, effective approach to learning contemporary prayer that works. This book positively impacted me and has advanced my own prayer work. A highly recommended read for anyone of any faith."—Tom Zender, Former President & CEO, Unity

"Thank you for your book . . . I didn't know it then, but I believe it is what has prepared me for this moment in my life . . . I am having major surgery tomorrow morning,. I am not scared, afraid, or nervous at all because I am convinced that as His child I am already completely and fully healed and that as His offspring He will not allow more harm to come to me.—Kristan Stanton, Houston, TX

I ordered this book for my husband as he was going through some tough times with work. I knew he would read it as he was already enjoying your Tuck In Prayers on Facebook. Of all the books I have given him, this is one that he actually read and has come to treasure. The clearly written, heart-felt prayers were just what he needed to bring him back to his own prayer practice. What was unexpected was how much joy and peace I received in reading it first! I am so grateful for this book,! Nancy Sogliuzzo, Writer/Artist San Diego, CA

Table of Contents

My Covenant

I will sing Your Praises when the morning comes and
when the night surrounds me.
My voice will be an instrument of healing to the
world.
I will let the light within me shine so that all who are
drawn to its light will be filled with the Holy Spirit.
Their ears will be open to the symphony of truth, and
their souls will know the Living God.
I am the keys upon which You play the music of life,
and the strings that quiver with resonating joy.
Let every breath be a melody that sings the eternal.
I am willing to sing Your song.

Gratitude

I am grateful to my first true prayer teacher, Rev. Lafayette Seymour, for demonstrating and living a Life of Prayer.

I am grateful to my children for giving me so many opportunities to pray and see it manifest through them.

I am grateful for my "Sista-Friends" for loving me while releasing me to do what I am here to do.

I am grateful for the situations, circumstances and people who provided me many opportunities to master the process of Prayer.

I am grateful to the Holy Spirit for all the wisdom, guidance, gifts and insights that have directed and supported me along this journey.

Thank you, God. You know why.

To Cindy Farris, one of the most brilliant women I have ever met, whose diligent review, proofreading and recommendations made this new edition even better than I could have hoped for, my deepest gratitude. I appreciate you so much girlfriend. I couldn't' have made this happen without you. I love you.

Forgiveness

I offer to myself full and absolute forgiveness for any and all error thought, misperception and unloving words and actions that have delayed my complete surrender to Divine Spirit and prevented the totally aligned relationship with God that has always existed within me as divine potential. I forgive myself.

I apologize to my body for the erroneous beliefs, and negative thoughts, words and actions that caused each and every activity of dis-ease and less than perfect health it has experienced as a result. Please forgive me.

I offer to my brothers and sisters, and every living thing upon the planet, my apology for any and all erroneous beliefs about you that were not in alignment with what I know to be the Truth of your being—that you are all perfect creations of God. I apologize for every error thought, unloving word, unkind act and violent emotions I have directed toward you or held within me about you. I apologize for each moment in which I believed we were separate and behaved accordingly. I apologize for failing to recognize your calls for love. Please forgive me.

I offer to my brothers and sisters everywhere my total forgiveness for every thought, word, action and feeling directed toward me that I perceived to be attack of any kind. I acknowledge your calls for love. I forgive you.

I offer my apologies to Mother Earth, and every living creature whose very existence makes this a beautiful planet, for my participation in any action that has brought harm upon them of any kind or for not taking a stand to assure their continued existence.

Please forgive me.

Introduction

I always knew that I would either write a part two to this book or have a revised version published. How did I know this? Because I know me . . .

I am always growing and expanding; I have a curious mind that is constantly seeking to know more about what I have already learned and to discover things I've never known before. Also, unashamedly, I admit that I get bored because of that curious mind. I love surprises; I love adventure; I love discovering new things and I embrace and enjoy the benefits of change.

The First Edition was written in 2003, nine years ago, and I am *so* not the person I was then. Many things have transpired in my life that have propelled me toward new dimensions in my spiritual growth and transformed the very fabric of my life and my being.

My former husband and I moved to Sacramento, California when he was hired as Senior Minister for Christ Unity Church; I compiled my EmpowerMag columns into a second book; I discovered and became enamored of Quantum Physics; I began to receive numerous invitations to speak at Unity Churches throughout California and in several places around the United States; I became an Interfaith Minister; I founded a phenomenal multicultural gospel choir; I discovered Radical Forgiveness and became certified to coach, teach and facilitate its concepts and techniques; I retired from Opera; I created a one-year program based on the Radical Empowerment Program that attracted a few hundred people for four years; my husband left the marriage giving me 18 hours notice; I released the gospel choir to its next leader; I polished and perfected my speaking skills; I totally forgave my former husband for everything; I moved to Walnut Creek, California to take a position at Unity Center of Walnut Creek as an Assistant Minister and Music Director under Senior Minister Rev. David McArthur; and I am republishing this book.

Wow!

Through the journey since the first edition of this book, I have explored my joy and my pain and discovered; (1) this amazing relationship with my Creator that has connected me with a profound wisdom, which is accessible to me as I surrender and am willing to move out of the way and simply allow; (2) this powerful, talented, creative, funny, beautiful, loyal, supportive and brilliant woman called "Me" that I not only love but like so very much; and (3) that I must not, no, cannot, allow anyone or anything to tempt me to diminish myself in any way; for, to do so diminishes the power of the expression of God as it flows through me and diminishes the purpose for which I was put on this planet:

> *To awaken and empower all humanity for*
> *the healing of the planet.*

Not only has my entire life changed, but my prayer life has changed—my awareness of what prayer is and how it works has expanded and taken a quantum leap. This new edition was, therefore, calling me to write it.

So here it is, a newly expanded version of *Praying Through a Storm: How Prayer Works—How to Make it Work for You.*

My son, Stephen (the one who manifested the computer at age 12), encouraged me to update and republish this book. He feels at this time, even more than at other times, greater numbers of people are in the midst of both personal and collective storms. Many are searching for something to hold onto that will keep them from being blown away.

It was also my desire because there is so much more to say about how I see prayer based on my personal "storm" experiences since the first book.

Some new components have been added to this edition; such as: Study Questions, A Pause for Reflection, a chapter on G.O.D (the Grand Operational Design) and an entire chapter on Quantum Prayer. Of course, I have expanded the other chapters with new information, new insights and new stories and examples of prayer working in my life and in the lives of family, friends, students, clients, readers and even my Facebook friends. You'll also find testimonies from people whose lives have been impacted by this book.

Turn the page and begin your journey. I know there is something here for you and I pray that when your storm comes this little book will provide a place of shelter for you.

Be blessed! Be bold! Be brave!

Sheila

Why Write a Book About Prayer?
(Introduction to the First Edition)

For as long as I can remember, ministers, priests, rabbis and other spiritual leaders have been saying "Let us pray." Then we would collectively bow our heads while words were offered to what we had been taught was God, the "person" who listened and determined our fate. We waited with great anticipation for our prayers to be answered, or we waited with great trepidation for our punishment.

At home, in the morning, or before bed, we would offer up our Lord's Prayer or such other prayer as taught by the tradition of our particular theology—usually on our knees. Then we waited with great anticipation for our prayers to be answered or, we waited with great trepidation for our punishment.

We never questioned these practices or the prayers that were spoken. They were the traditions of our family and places of worship, and we pretty much did what we were told.

But what is prayer? Who, exactly are we praying to? Why do we pray? What happens to those prayers that are never answered? Is there one way to pray that works all the time?

These questions plagued me for many years, and for many years I did not pray at all. I had been taught that we were "born in sin and shaped in iniquity" and that we were doomed to hell. I figured "what the heck, I'll just go party since I'm going to hell anyway." And . . . Boy, did I ever!!

It took a very serious illness to get me praying again, as may be the case for many people.

For almost four years I wrote columns for EmpowerMag.com, an internet magazine that features writers who offer principles, guidelines and tools for self-empowerment. At the end of my column, *Message for the Miracle-Minded*, I always offered a prayer as a way of sealing the message in consciousness. I began receiving e-mails from many readers suggesting that I publish a book of my prayers. My husband suggested that I expand upon the idea and write a book about prayer, because of my effective and highly successful transformational classes and training programs for prayer partners.

That is how this book began—but not really. It actually began and has been writing itself, over the last ten years, as I made discoveries along my own personal prayer journey and as I weathered many storms in my own life. What I teach is what I have learned about my own prayer life and what I have been teaching others. The teaching has only served to solidify, expand and strengthen what prayer is and has been for me.

This is a book about prayer, but prayers themselves are much more effective when we understand the spiritual principles and scientific laws that govern the orderly process of prayer and that assure their ultimate fulfillment in the manifest realm.

Before I learned the orderly process of universal law and how it played out in bringing forth our desires or answers to our prayers, it was very perplexing to me that some of my prayers were answered and some were not.

In my Baptist and Methodist background, we were taught that God only answered our prayers if we were good and did not sin. I figured that must have been the reason why some of my prayers were not answered—I must have done something God didn't like and He decided I didn't deserve to get what I wanted. I was pretty content with that until I was led to New Thought theology.

In my first Unity experiences we were taught that *all* prayers are answered. This, however, only served to further perplex me because all of my prayers *still* weren't being answered.

As I began to study metaphysical courses, it became clear that prayer was more than an activity—it was a process—and by understanding the process and praying in alignment with the process, my prayers were answered to the degree by which I adhered to the process.

But the "process" is more than merely steps for practicing a method to get a result. The process itself is actually founded on provable scientific principles. It is important to understand what prayer is and how it works if we are to see our prayers answered in the manifest realm as we intended.

Here, in this little book, I offer you my discoveries and some of the prayers that have been placed upon my heart by the Holy Spirit to help you get started.

Prayer, for most of us, was a desperate S.O.S. reserved for special occasions. We thought we were praying only when addressing God directly with some screech for "HELP!" But since Energy is the force field that runs the universe, every thought we have is a prayer.

Pam Grout
God Doesn't Have Bad Hair Days

What is Prayer?

Into every life storms come; they may even manifest as a Hurricane Katrina or tornado, decimating and devastating everything in its path within our body of affairs.

As they bear down upon us, it may appear that the roof of our faith has blown away and the walls of our courage have caved in, while the waters are rising and we are drowning in fear.

On a purely physical level, these storms are often very painful and may cause us to feel isolated and alone. We may even feel a depth of despair that triggers depression and an unwillingness to go on any longer.

Yet, when the storms of life are raging and we find ourselves being beaten down by the winds and the pouring rain, from some place deep within us a spark of revelation may catch our attention in the midst of despair and compel us to cry out to an unseen source of hope to give us that last vestige of strength to take one more step and to draw one more breath.

That, my beloved, is prayer . . . in the spiritual sense.

Reading the original opening to this chapter gives me chills, as I reflect upon the last two years of my life that brought storm after storm after storm, and I realize I never would have made it had not been for, not only the Truth teachings that were part of my life for the past thirty-four years in Unity, but also having taken them on as a way of life and teaching them to others. But . . . I digress . . .

Let us take a closer look at this thing called *Prayer* and approach it from an intellectual as well as a scientific perspective to get a foundation for ourselves in comprehending the mechanisms that form the operating system of Prayer, for it is the *knowledge* of something that makes us masters of it.

For study purposes, it appears there are as many definitions of prayer as there are prayers. Although many writers and teachers have their individual definitions of prayer, you will discover that they still come to the same general conclusion and, ultimately, you will form your own definition of prayer if you have not done so already.

> *Prayer is the most highly accelerated mind action known. It steps up mental action until man's consciousness synchronizes with the Christ Mind. It is the language of spirituality; when developed, it makes man master in the realm of creative ideas.*[1]

Charles Fillmore, co-founder of Unity Worldwide Ministries, is telling us that prayer is the activity of mind that creates a direct link with our Creator and engages our ability to draw from the realm of all knowledge that which we desire to have manifested into visible expression. He says it, in effect, makes us Masters of the Universe©.

---

[1] Charles R. Fillmore, *The Revealing Word* (Missouri: Unity Books 1994), p. 152.

We might compare prayer with the umbilical cord that connects the unborn fetus with the mother. It is through the umbilical cord that the fetus is nourished and nurtured *in utero* to grow to full term and be born as a completely functioning human being, expressing itself through all of its senses and organs and mastering the ability to survive on its own.

Through prayer, *we* are nourished and nurtured so that we might come into the fullness of life and express the power of the Source from which we are formed.

> *Prayer is a conscious expression of the upward trend of nature found everywhere . . . every impulse or desire of the soul for life, love and light, is a prayer.*[2]

In other words, prayer takes us from the three-dimensional realm of probability to the fourth-dimensional realm of possibility or potential. We can only achieve conscious union with God through the conscious activity of prayer. By unifying our consciousness with Divine Mind, we connect with that Truth of our being that releases us from the necessity of pain, suffering and struggle.

Prayer is mental activity that opens the way for our spiritual approach to the physical experience of God.

When we pray, we tap into the heart center where we connect with Divine Mind for a first-person experience with that from which we evolved; and we are quickened with the life force that sustains the universe and every heart that beats.

---

[2] Charles & Cora Fillmore; *Teach Us To Pray* (Missouri: Unity Books 1959), Foreword.

Have you ever prayed and found yourself weeping tenderly in the midst of your prayer? That is the heart connection with Spirit that moves us to a sacred experience. When praying about a challenge or condition in our lives, we feel a sense of relief, peace and expectancy when this connection is made.

In 1998, my daughter Sian was in a very serious automobile accident, causing a closed head injury that left her in a coma. When I heard the news I was in SEE Classes (Spiritual Education and Enrichment, formerly CEP—Continuing Education Program) in Chicago to earn my Licensed Unity Teacher credentials. Coincidentally, or should I say *synchronisticly*, I was in a class called "Life of Prayer." I was in the second day of classes and would lose all of the tuition fees paid for the week if I left right away.

I was torn by a mother's desire to be with my daughter and the desire to get the classes I needed in order to do the work God was telling me to do. At the end of the telephone call from New Jersey, I went into the meditation garden there and prayed. I don't remember how long I sat there in prayer, but it was quite a long time. By the end of my prayer I had surrendered totally to God's Will and waited for guidance. After about an hour, I received only one word: "stay." I felt a sense of relief and release, and tears were rolling down my cheeks. There was a knowing that God would be there with my daughter and that I would arrive at exactly the time I needed to be there.

I returned to my class, related what had happened and asked the instructor and students to pray with me and with Sian. Rev. Terry Lund, our instructor, led us in prayer and wc continued to pray throughout the week.

4

My husband (now former) was Chaplain at what was then called Unity School for Religious Studies and asked the Ministerial Candidates, instructors and staff to pray for Sian. He also asked the Silent Unity staff to put her on their prayer list. The students began sending out prayer requests for her all over the world and, literally, thousands of people began praying for her recovery.

When I did arrive at my daughter's bedside at the end of the week, she came out of the coma shortly after I entered her hospital room. When I entered the room, there was a golden egg-shaped field of energy surrounding her bed, and I knew that it was the energy field caused by the thousands of prayer offerings being sent in her direction.

Prayer is an activity of the heart that simplifies the complex. We have spent lifetimes studying the complexities of our lives in order to break them down to a level of understanding. Prayer demonstrates the simplicity of life by setting up a pure flow of energy dynamics before us that reveal the oneness and sameness of everything and opens a pathway that guides us through the maze.

As a child, I was 100% in the heart. I loved everybody and everybody loved me. I was very smart but was totally disinterested in intellectual pursuits. I made really good grades without studying. I only wanted to sing, dance, read mysteries and write. In my 30s I was led to Unity by a life-threatening illness and Metaphysics opened up a part of my brain that began to hunger for the deeper intellectual concepts of the Science of Being and led to an obsession with Quantum Mechanics.

Now, having reached an amazing balance between intellect and spirituality, I have found that I can comprehend the depths of a subject with the mind and then simplify it with the heart for the purpose of making it palatable for those I teach. I learn it and bring it to prayer within the heart and it becomes crystal clear.

> *True prayer brings about an exalted radiation of energy and, when it is accompanied by faith, judgment and love, the word of Truth bursts forth in a stream of light that, when held in mind, illumines, uplifts and glorifies.*[3]

This "exalted radiation of energy" is more deeply impressed upon our mind, body and consciousness when we understand how prayer works.

Prayer is the activating inner key. It sends out the vibrations of thoughts from our heart. Through prayer we make a statement about what we align and work with, and that is the movement of our own limitations.

Prayer is the process that calms us amid the storm and assures us that the sun will shine again.

---

[3] Charles R. Fillmore, *Atom Smashing Power of Mind* (Missouri: Unity Books 1949), p. 40.

Prayers become real to us when the emotion behind them, within them, is so strong that the prayer becomes animated—it has life.

O. Hallesby

How Does Prayer Work?

Most people I know pray and, since September 11, 2001 and in the midst of the recent activities of wars, international economic collapse, tsunamis, earthquakes, Katrina, the BP oil spill and more wars, many more people have returned to the comforting activity and experience of prayer to find some way of achieving hope and promise in the midst of world chaos.

But how many of us really know how prayer works? We close our eyes, fold our hands and say the words. But then what?

We have been told that our prayers go to a great *Being* out there somewhere, who hears them and determines whether or not we are worthy of having them answered. Sort of like Santa Claus, who checks his list twice to find out who has been naughty or nice. It sounds to me like we would stand a better chance with rolling a set of dice and hoping for a "7."

I remember reading an article in which the author suggested a parallel of going back in time and giving baseball equipment to the cavemen without instructions in how to use the equipment or the rules of the game. This was an important analogy, because we tell people *to* pray but do not teach them *how* to pray or enlighten them about the way our prayers work. There are many aspects of prayer, when learned and understood, that take our prayers to another level.

Prayer is extremely powerful, but it does not respond only to our pleas (words). It responds to every intention—conscious and unconscious—with opposing sides battling it out.

Prayer is also not an activity of chance or luck or worthiness. Prayer is based on the scientific laws of energy. It is an actual energy expressing outward into the realm of matter. It is the medium through which we affect cause upon that energy in order to produce the highest level of manifestation: answered prayer.

Science has proven that there is a universal life force called "energy" that animates and sustains all the forms and shapes of the universe. Since splitting the atom, scientists have determined that it is charged with tremendous energy. This energy may be utilized by us for earthly powers beyond our wildest imagination when used in alignment with the laws governing that energy. Science has proven that this energy is contained within *all* matter.

A drop of water, for example, contains enough power (energy) to blow up a ten-story building.

Scientists have come to understand the mental and spiritual abilities within us that provide us with the power to develop and release these energies that are stored within the cells of our physical bodies and the construct of our minds.

Prayer utilizes this energy through the Law of Mind Action. This Law is the process through which prayer manifests that for which we pray. The Law of Mind Action states: *"Thoughts held in mind produce after their kind."*

This Law of Mind Action operates by three methods:

Oneness—God is one with all creation. We function, and our lives manifest, out of that oneness. As the mind of each of us is one with God-Mind, the mind of each of us is connected.

For example, if you take a bucket of water out of the ocean, it still contains all of the attributes of the ocean; therefore, it is still the ocean. We are, therefore, still very much a part of God just as the ocean water is still part of the ocean. Our bodies are simply buckets filled with God.

Order—The right sequence of events is established. We live in an orderly universe, and that which we send out into it works under its *orderly* principles and laws. There are no accidents or coincidences. It is often referred to as "right timing."

For example, if you start a tulip garden and place the bulbs on top of the ground, the likelihood of a beautiful and lush garden is very slim; however, if you till the soil, dig a hole in the dirt to receive the bulbs, in an orderly manner, when spring arrives you will have beautiful tulips to show for it.

The Universe works in the same manner and responds to our preparation for its orderly outworking.

There are times when it appears our prayers are not being answered in a timely manner. This simply means that it has not completed its orderly process. We must continue to do our part and trust that *divine timing* is playing out and our request will manifest in the fullness of time.

Circulation—Divine ideas and divine substance constantly circulate from the unmanifest realm (God) to the manifest realm and back to the unmanifest realm. Circulation governs all creation and its primary functions (breathing, blood flow, etc.). Circulation always brings us more of whatever we circulate.

Using the example of your tulip garden, if you plant only sunflower seeds, don't expect tulips when spring comes. If you want tulips, you must plant tulip bulbs.

So it follows that, if your thoughts, feelings and emotions are consistently filled with fear, doubt, unworthiness and lack, you can be certain that your life will reflect corresponding conditions

The Law of Mind Action, therefore, will produce for us that which we intend and that with which we align our consciousness or thoughts.

But there is more to how thought operates. In order for our thoughts to have the energy to create, they must be given firepower.

Gregg Braden, in the *Isaiah Effect*, says "thought alone has little energy; it is only a possibility with no energy to give it life."[4]

Therefore, we must add fuel to thought—emotion. Without emotion, thought has no power to make itself real. Without emotion, we can look at life and its inherent possibilities without miscreation.

Linked to thought is Imagination. When we imagine our creations, our thoughts bring them to life.

When we add Love or its opposite, Fear, to thought, "we breathe life into the creations of our imagination."[5]

---

[4] Gregg Braden, *The Isaiah Effect* (New York: Harmony Books 2000), p. 150.
[5] Ibid.

Fillmore says: *prayer is the opening of communication between the mind of man and the mind of God. Prayer is the exercise of faith in the presence and power of the <u>unseen</u> God.*[6]

The *unseen God* Fillmore is speaking about is that energy which undergirds and permeates everything.

While there are many definitions for prayer, we can sum it up very simply: Prayer is energy expressing.

So, let's look at what could be the scientific formula for this energy when applied to prayer.

FEELING X (EMOTION + THOUGHT) = POWER

Please note, this is what I call a *Sheilaism*. There is absolutely no scientific formula for prayer that I know of; this is something I made up when designing a training program for Prayer Partners in order to support them in really understanding what truly activates prayer.

What does this formula mean? Let's look first at some definitions for the components of the formula to shed some light on it.

Emotion

1. an affective state of consciousness in which joy, sorrow, fear, hate, or the like, is experienced, as distinguished from cognitive and volitional states of consciousness.[7]

---

[6] Charles R. Fillmore, *Atom Smashing Power of Mind* (Missouri: Unity Books 1949), p. 11.
[7] Webster's Unabridged Dictionary of the English Language.

11

Essentially, what Webster's definition is saying is that it is not of the mind (an intellectual choice or decision) but of the heart (an experience). We might say that *Emotion* is the source of power that drives us forward toward our goals in life and fuels our thoughts to make them real.

Metaphysically, emotions are defined as "undisciplined or uncontrolled forces; subnormal or supernormal activity of mental or physical forces; excitement of the feelings.[8]

We have two primary emotions—Love and Fear. Love is the most profound emotion of all; it is the First Cause of all existence and is the power behind divine expression. Anything we experience as the opposite of Love is the other emotion—Fear.

Although an emotion may show up as doubt, mistrust, unforgiveness, hate, anger, anxiety, loneliness, etc., they are all sub-emotions of Fear.

For example: If we are in doubt about something, it simply means that we fear our own divine judgment. Within each of us is the ability to see the Truth behind all things and make a Spiritual Judgment based on Divine Wisdom.

Linked to Emotion is Desire, which is the force that sparks our imagination to resolution.

In the Movie *What the Bleep Do We Know* it was said: "Emotions themselves are not bad—they are life—it is our addictions that are the problem. Emotions use the same neuro-receptors as heroin addiction.

---

[8] Fillmore; Revealing Word

In other words, we are addicted to certain emotions; such as fear, anger, jealousy and hatred. There is a certain hunger that they feed and these neuro-receptors begin to crave the euphoria they bring and we draw to us situations that trigger those emotions.

Emotions alone are directionless. Thought provides the direction to our emotions and the emotions bring the vitalizing force to the images expressed from within our thoughts.

Thought

1. *An idea or opinion produced by thinking;*
2. *A picture imagined and contemplated.* [9]

Thought, therefore, is an activity of the brain that produces concepts, ideas, opinions and imagination. Thoughts are like non-verbal communication.

Thought is the guidance system that directs Emotion. It is the ideas created by thought that determine the direction of our emotions and attention.

Metaphysically, thought represents a "mental vibration or impulse, having an identity that encompasses a central ego, around which all its elements revolve; thoughts are things." [10]

Thoughts are energy currents that, when moved through the creative structure of mind, connect with all the similar energy currents in the universe. They then mold a collective consciousness that returns to us amplified to the trillionth

---

[9] Webster's Unabridged Dictionary of the English Language.

[10] Fillmore, <u>Revealing Word</u>

power and manifest into visible tangible matter in our body of affairs.

As we pray verbally or in thought, the energy of our words and thoughts goes out into the magnetic ethers, searches for the corresponding energy, gathers it together and returns to create the realization of the original thoughts or words. First comes the idea, and then the expression.

In other words, our thoughts go out into the neighborhood of Thoughtville, gather up all their little friends and bring them home to us for a play date. They bring happiness, fun and joy to add greater beauty to our lives or drain our resources, stay past their welcome and wreak havoc upon our abode (body/life).

When we think of something we don't have to actually say it because it has been projected by way of our thought itself. Just because we don't actually say it doesn't mean it has any less power.

You may have heard the expression "every thought is a prayer." If you want to know what you have been praying, look around you at your current life situation. What your thought system has been will be revealed to you. What do you see? Do you like what you see? If not, you can transform your life by aligning your thoughts and prayers with the goodness of Spirit.

Feeling

1) *generalized body consciousness or sensation; the function or the power of perceiving.*
2) *physical sensation not connected with sight, hearing, taste, or smell;*

3) *An emotional state or reaction.*[11]

From this definition, we can determine that our perception shapes the feelings we experience as a result of what we see. Feelings, then, are the outer expression of an inner perception.

Metaphysically, Charles Fillmore defines feeling as "external to thought." He says: *behind every feeling or emotion there lies thought, which is its direct cause. To erase a feeling, a change of thought is required.*[12]

Feeling is the key to prayer. It is the energy to which creation responds, representing the union of Thought and Emotion, and may only exist in their combined presence.

Feelings assist us in determining why we attract certain people, situations and conditions into our lives.

Gregg Braden says "when we have a Feeling, "we are experiencing the desire of our emotion merged with the imagination of our thoughts."[13]

The *intention* within the context of our thoughts, backed by the *feelings* attached to that intention, acts as a catalyst for propelling the prayer's energy into the "unseen force," which activates the formation of the molecular activity of Creation/Manifestation.

In other words, *feeling* is the prayer itself.

While we may use powerful words to express prayer, the outward manifestation of the request will not express itself

---

[11] Webster's Unabridged Dictionary of the English Language.

[12] Fillmore, <u>Revealing Word</u>.

[13] Gregg Braden, *The Isaiah Effect* (New York: Harmony Books 2000), p. 150.

until we align our thoughts and feelings with the words we pray. If we are to transform the conditions of the outer, we must become within ourselves the "intention" of our prayer requests.

In an online article, Walter Last says of feelings:

> *Feelings provide us with the greatest pleasures in life, but also with the greatest suffering. Suffering actually is the key word for our loss of feeling with advancing age. We do not want to suffer, so we intentionally diminish our feelings in order to diminish the amount of emotional pain that we do feel. As an unintended side effect this also reduces the amount of pleasure that we can feel.*[14]

Now, you may be asking: "What's the difference between *feeling* and *emotion*? Good question. It is one frequently asked by students and workshop participants.

Emotions are born within the solar plexus. They are strongly felt energies that compel us to action; for example, anger is an emotion that causes us to have an urge to <u>do</u> something.

Feelings, on the other hand, are born of the heart and are an experience. When they arise, we simply want to <u>be</u>. For example, feelings of love and peace inspire within us a desire to simple experience them.

We also *feel* the emotions that arise; however, that feeling is rooted in the lower chakras. True *feelings* are upper chakra experiences. Furthermore, there is a certain aspect

---

[14] Walter Last; The World of Feelings and Emotions; www.health-science-spirit.com/feelings.html.

of *intuition* connected to *feelings.* Have you ever heard someone say, "I had a *feeling* she was going to call" or "I had a *feeling* I shouldn't have taken that route?" Our *intuition* and *insights* frequently show up as a *feeling.* Finally, Love can be both a *feeling* and an *emotion,* depending upon whether it emanates from the heart of from the solar plexus.

Having this awareness, how would this formula play out in our lives?

Applying the Formula

FEELING X (EMOTION + THOUGHT) = POWER

When we add the emotion of love to our thoughts about God and about the desires of our hearts, then multiply it by feelings of trust, belief, oneness and knowing, the power of prayer is activated and the manifestation is assured.

Let's apply this to a life situation.

Diana has been praying for the right and perfect job but she hasn't quite been able to kick-start any energy or movement around it. If she were to use the formula, it might look like this:

Appreciation x (Desire + Vision of Perfect Job) Employment

As she allows feelings of appreciation for the job in which she is currently employed to rise up in her heart, being grateful for her co-workers and a steady income, while holding a vision of the job she truly desires, a strong channel of potential is activated within the Universe and the power of God's ever-present willingness to provide creates the outcome of the original intention.

At one time in my life I was working as a free-lance Legal Secretary and Word Processor to earn money to help with the expenses of living in New York City while pursuing an opera career and the expenses of the best voice teachers and coaches. During one period of time, I was contracting with one Law Firm exclusively and would show up each day to either be placed with one of the attorneys or to work in the Word Processing Center for the day.

There was one particular partner no one wanted to work for; not because of him but because of the group of secretaries whose desks were in the same area as his secretary. One day, it was my misfortune (fortune) to be placed there not only for the day but throughout the period of his secretary's recovery from major surgery. It was determined that she would probably be out a few months. OMG! I immediately wondered what I had done to deserve such a punishment.

Sure enough, my first day was hell and the three of them were their usual *itchy* selves and made my life miserable. Day after day, I would get up in the morning grumbling about having to go there to work and day after day I had the same experience. Somehow, through the *Course in Miracles* group I was facilitating weekly, I received the wisdom to be grateful for where I was if there was going to be any movement toward getting me out of there. I created an affirmation: "I love the work I do and the people I work with; I am loving and they are loving too." I said it every day, eventually even making up a melody for it and dancing to it. One day, I received a call from an organization in Harlem that had gotten funding to create a Welfare-to-Work Program and offered me a $10,000 contract to design the computer training aspect and the training materials. Hello!

By holding appreciation in my heart for where I was and multiplying the strong desire to have something that truly fulfilled me, the inner power to co-create with God took over and I was propelled toward a successful outcome.

When I announced my departure, the three other secretaries cried and hugged me. We had become a team, helping each other and bringing in treats and being supportive to those whose workload was greater than the rest. Did they change? Absolutely not! My willingness to "appreciate" transformed my experience and manifested what I desired.

Through this formula, Prayer serves the purpose for which it is expressed.

When our storms come, we can use prayer as a provable formula to align our thoughts, feelings and emotions with spiritual Truth and experience an assurance that we have the power to ride out the bad weather.

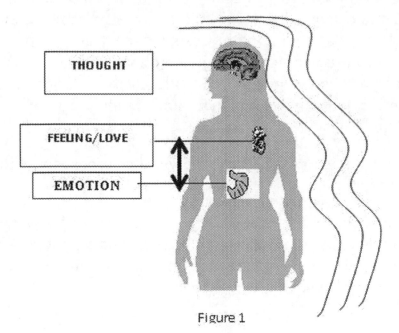

Figure 1

In Figure 1, we see where the energies of Thought Feeling and Emotion are centered within the human body and how they directly affect the field of energy that surrounds us.

*Prayer, for most of us, was a desperate S.O.S. reserved for special occasions. We thought we were **praying** only when addressing God directly with some screech for "HELP!" But since [Energy] is the force field that runs the universe, every thought we have is a prayer.*[15]

Who/What Do We Pray To?

In our desperation to know and understand God, we have anthropomorphized (given human characteristics to) it into a powerful male bearded facsimile of our own human construct, who sits on a throne-like chair and hands out punishment and rewards in accordance with his determination of the "goodness" or "badness" of our behavior. We have heaped upon this Creator the responsibility for our fortune or misfortune as the case may be, and we have trained ourselves to live in fear and trepidation of what may befall us if we make him angry.

Our attachment to the three-letter identity in which we have cast this powerful entity has caused us to place serious limitations on the vast expansiveness of this omnipotent, omniscient and omnipresent source of all that is. By limiting it to G-O-D, we are unable to comprehend the true majesty and magnificence of that which we call *"God."*

If we are bible students, we would know that nowhere in the bible does our Creator say "call me God." In fact, when Moses was instructed to free the Israelites from Egypt, he asked: *But what should I say, if they ask me your name?* And he was told: *Tell them that the LORD, whose name is "I Am," has sent you. This is my name forever, and it is the name that people must use from now on.*[16]

---

[15] Pam Grout, *God Doesn't Have Bad Hair Days* (Pennsylvania: Running Press 2005), p. 57.

[16] Exodus 3:13 Contemporary English Version (CEV)

The God of Adam and Eve, of Moses and Abraham, Isaac and Jacob called itself "I Am."

In other words, "I am not reducible to the minimalized expectations and imagination of your limited point of reference. I Am. You cannot confine me, define me or comprehend my scope and magnitude. I Am.

In that identity is the allness and fullness of that which is the sum and substance of everything created and yet to be created.

So, who or what do we pray to?

In Unity and other New Thought theologies, we refer to God in many ways: Mother-Father God, Infinite Presence, Divine Presence and other non-religious references. We do so, in order to open up the relationship with God to all people—not merely Christian males—and support them in feeling that God is the God of all races, genders, beliefs, political affiliations and sexual designations.

God is both our Mother and Father. God has no gender. God is both immanent (within, near) and transcendent (everywhere present). This is very important for all of us to embrace if we are to stop the conflict that arises from religious affiliations and doctrines.

Remember that, in the encounter with Moses, It did not put a "what" following "I Am." This means that it is whatever we put after "I Am . . ."

I Am: Love, Pure Light, Life, Abundance, Wholeness, Peace, Power, Healing, Joy, etc.

If this is true, then who or what do we pray to?

We pray to an all-loving, all-good, all-powerful, everywhere-present, all-providing substance that can be called the "**G**rand **O**perational **D**esign."

In Quantum Physics, it is referred to as the Quantum Field—the space where all possibility exists; the birthplace of all atoms and molecules; the source of everything before it manifests as matter and to which it returns.

This field is composed of the same energy particles of which we are made and in our daily lives we interact with this field through our thoughts, words, feelings and emotions.

We are one with this Grand Operational Design and it is one with us. Our very beingness impacts the totality of all that is part of or connected to this field.

In fact, the more we seek to know God the more God expands. Based on Quantum Physics, the more we explore the universe the more it expands.

What we pray to is the essence born of this field known as "Self" and is the Divine Aspect of us. So when we pray we do not pray to change God's mind; we pray to change our mind about the goodness, lovingness, generous nature of God from the part of us that is connected to It.

God does not need our prayers; God has already provided everything we could ever possibly need, require or desire. All that makes up the Kingdom of God has been given to us. It exists in that unseen realm of substance and awaits the expansion of our consciousness to arrive at a point of acceptance to manifest in our lives as Reality.

This might cause us to wonder why it is necessary to pray at all.

The purpose of prayer is to integrate the attributes of God into [our] consciousness which, in turn, will manifest as corresponding conditions.[17]

J. Douglas Bottorf

What is the Purpose of Prayer?

In Truth, there really is no need to pray; God already knows our every need. In fact, God knows the need before the asking, because God places the desire upon our hearts in the first place. When we pray, we pray to have a realization of what is already the Absolute Truth; so, we pray to change *our* minds not God's because God doesn't need our prayers. We do!

Remember when Jesus raised Lazarus? He said "Father, I thank thee that thou hast heard me. I knew that thou hearest me always, but I have said this on account of the people standing by, that they may believe that thou didst send me." (John 11:41-42)

He was really saying. "Look, I don't really have to ask for this, 'cause you already know the situation here; but, because these people don't know who they are and what they are capable of, I'll just ask for their benefit. Okay?"

God puts desires upon our hearts to remind us that the Kingdom of Heaven is available to us as soon as we align ourselves with the Holy Spirit and believe that everything we need, require and desire is ours as a gift from our Creator.

---

[17] J. Douglas Bottorf, *A Practical Guide to Meditation and Prayer* (Missouri: Unity Books 1990), p.61.

Everything we "pray" about eventually externalizes. Our inner thoughts are continually being cut and pasted into our outer life.

If you want to know what you are really "praying" for, take a look around your life. You'll see your innermost thoughts, the real desires of your heart, the prayers no one knows about but you (your unconscious self).

> *We do not pray to conquer God's reluctance to give; we pray to align ourselves with God's willingness to give.*[18]

Prayer opens a communication link between our mind and Divine Mind. Through this link, there is a transfer of energy and God becomes our "silent partner".

In this partnership, we work within the realm of substance to "bring forth" as our Creator did in the creation of the world, and we manifest to the degree of our faith.

We pray to align ourselves with the promises of God and to become one with the Grand Operational Design (G.O.D.) that has already established a thing for us and awaits our acceptance of it in the manifest realm.

So, the purpose of prayer then is to consciously create—actually co-create—in perfect alignment with G.O.D. so what we really desired is what is externalized as manifest reality.

> *The power of prayer can bring forth the greatest powers of transformation. Prayers generate energy patterns which are used as a direct bio-coupling frequency by the Divine, activating levels of Light transformation within us and connecting us directly with the higher emanations and*

---

[18] Author unknown.

hierarchies that can lead us, as Christ led Pistis Sophia, directly into an intimate Divine experience. [19]

The purpose of prayer is to practice the presence of God until we are able to know it personally through experience and live in that presence with certainty that it exists and is providing for us at every moment. In other words, until we have faith.

---

[19] Pistis Sophia, p. 475

PAUSE FOR REFLECTION & STUDY

At this time I invite you to take some time to reflect on what you have read so far, if you wish, and allow these concepts to settle within your heart and your mind. If you are part of a Book Study Group, this may be a good time for discussion. Below are some Study Questions to assist you:

 What is your personal definition of prayer?

 How does prayer align our minds with the flow of the universe?

 Is prayer a passive or an active verb?

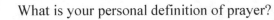 Reflect upon, or discuss in your group, what "practicing the presence of God" and "practicing spiritual principles" means to you.

How have you seen the Law of Mind Action play out in your life? What was the result?

Does the subconscious mind know when we are joking?

Is the purpose of prayer to change one's self or to attain conscious oneness with God?

If there is no need to pray, what is the point of praying? What would we do instead?

Faith stands firmly rooted in all-pervading love and life, unshaken by doubt and death.[20]

William J. Bennett

What is Faith?

"Faith is the perceiving power of the mind linked with the power to shape substance."[21]

Faith is "a firm belief in something for which there is no proof; complete trust; something that is believed with strong conviction; without doubt or question."[22]

Faith is "spiritual assurance; power to do the seemingly impossible; magnetic power that draws unto us our heart's desire from the invisible spiritual substance."[23]

Fillmore further says: "Faith is more than mere belief. It is the very substance of that which is believed. It works by love. Thoughts of condemnation, enmity and resistance must be released and divine love declared; then faith will work unhindered."[24]

The energy we discussed in the last section must be directed, and Faith is the rocket booster that propels the Emotion that fires the imagination [thought] that creates the feeling that all is well and we are dwelling in our oneness with our First Cause.

---

[20] William J. Bennett, *The Book of Virtues* (New York: Simon & Schuster 1993), p.917.

[21] Charles R. Fillmore, *The Revealing Word* (Missouri: Unity Books 1959), p. 67.

[22] Webster's Ninth New Collegiate Dictionary, 1988 by Merriam-Webster.

[23] Fillmore, 1959, p. 67

[24] Ibid, p. 68

When Sian was in the coma following her accident, I never thought she would not come out of the coma. I knew, don't know how but I knew, that she would not only come out of that coma but would be alright in every other sense. I can honestly say that was only the second time in my spiritual journey that a degree of faith was being called for that was beyond anything I ever believed I was capable of achieving.

The Bible says, *"Faith is the substance of things hoped for; the evidence of things not seen. For by it the elders obtained a good report. By faith we understand that the ages were framed by a word of God, so that the things being seen not to have come into being out of the things that appear"*. (Heb 11:1-3)

What is Paul talking about here? What point is he trying to make?

First, faith is the *substance* of things hoped for. What is this thing called *substance?*

The word substance comes from the Latin word *substare—sub* meaning "up to, under" and *stare*, which means "to stand."

Faith is that which forms the foundation of manifestation; it stands up to its promises of rewards; and is the understanding that God/The Universe stands ready to provide everything we need, require and desire.

In other words, when we have faith, we are taking a stand and making a statement that we stand firm in our trust of God's willingness to provide.

Second, faith is *evidence* of things not seen. What have we here?

If you have ever been in a courtroom or watched one of the hundreds of courtroom dramas and reality shows on television, you have more than likely heard an attorney make a request to submit something into *evidence,* which is then followed by the Judge telling the bailiff to mark it as "Exhibit A."

Evidence is that which *proves* something, is it not? If that is the case, then faith is actually the *proof* that something is possible. It is the proof that we trust God to take care of things.

To put it simply, when we have faith we are saying we have absolutely no doubt regarding the outcome.

Malachi 3:10 says, *"prove me now and see if I will not open up a window and pour you out a blessing that there will not be room enough to spare".*

In order to "prove God now" we must have faith in that unseen source of our supply.

That which is *unseen* is unseen because we have not yet proven that we have the consciousness to bring it into manifestation.

"When we direct the mental powers upon a definite idea, faith plays its part; it is involved in concentration. As we give attention to the idea through one-pointed mind concentration, we break into a realm of finer mind activity, called faith or the fire of Spirit. Thus faith opens the door into an inner consciousness, where we hold the

31

word steadily in mind until the spiritual ethers respond to our word. Earnest, steady, and continued attention along this line is bound to bring forth the fruits of the Spirit in abundant measure. A steady, unwavering devotion of heart and principle to Spirit develops in us supermind qualities."[25]

Prayer without faith is like an airplane without wings. Without the absolute assurance that your Source is <u>ever</u> ready to provide everything you need, require and desire, the prayer may take off but it has nothing to keep it afloat.

Faith is the *hotline* to our Christ consciousness. By utilizing this Power, our prayers evolve from mere appeals to manifestations of the deepest desires of the heart (God). In the midst of the raging storms of challenge even a momentary awareness of Faith, removes us from the vortex and transports us into the calm eye (IAM) where we reconnect with our Divinity and remember that as Gods we are always in concert with creative principle and, thus, have the Power to transcend above the condition to see the Truth which is always there. Faith is that invisible essence which provides the encouragement to our seeking souls to continue the journey for the treasure is at hand. Faith opens the door.

When our storms came, *faith* is the umbrella you carried even when the sun was shining. You knew it was going to rain at some point.

---

[25] Charles R. & Cora Fillmore; *Teach Us To Pray* (Missouri: Unity Books 1959), p. 33.

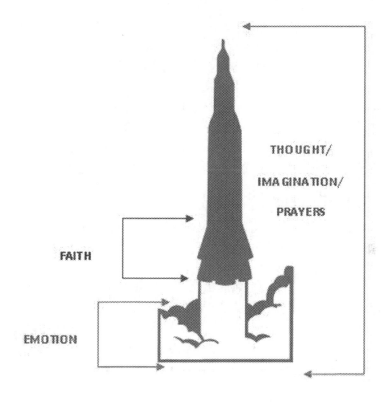

Figure 2

In Figure 2, we see our emotions powering up Faith so that our prayers can be launched into the invisible realm of substance where they are transmuted into manifest substance.

. . . faith is an affirmative attitude of mind that uses the creative power of thought constructively.[26]

Ernest Holmes

How Does Faith Work?

Figure 2 shows how faith propels our prayers. In the example, faith is the rocket booster that fires the rocket so that it has lift to take it off the ground and into the air where the other controls can take over and direct its mission.

It takes faith to get our prayers off the ground. Once they are in the energy, they are under the control of Spirit. Spirit will then direct their mission.

Many of us say we have faith, but do we really? How do we know we have faith? Without an opportunity to use our faith, we have only a *textbook* knowledge of that faith. When the challenge comes, and we stand upon our trust in God, then we have a *working* knowledge of faith.

Faith places the prayer in the realm of "Knowing," from which Jesus always extracted the power to manifest miracles into the present moment.

Faith is God's gift to [humankind], establishing an eternal bond between us and the power within, the power that created us . . . It acquaints us with the power that is hidden from the reasoning mind and reveals itself as a feeling of oneness with the eternal good."[27]

---

[26] Ernest Holmes, *Good for You*, (California: Science of Mind Publications 1987), p.1.

[27] May Rowland, *Dare to Believe* (Missouri: Unity Books 1951), p. 54-55.

One of the greatest demonstrations of faith I've ever witnessed came from my son, Stephen, when he was twelve years old.

Stephen wanted a computer badly. He decided he wanted an Apple IIe, and he decided upon all the features he wanted. He wrote them down. He then cleared a space on his desk and propped a picture of the computer against the wall behind his desk, where he would sit and pretend he was writing programs. He would take his allowance and buy all the computer magazines he could find. Every time he passed a computer store, he went in to look at them and ask endless questions of the salespeople.

Unfortunately, two things prevented Stephen from getting his computer; 1) We had no money (I was a single parent) and; 2) Apple was only manufacturing Apple IIe computers every two years and it would be another year before one was available. Stephen was disappointed but not deterred. He said he knew he was getting a computer. He kept visiting computer stores and leaving his name and telephone number in case they came across one.

One day Stephen received a call from a salesman at one of the computer stores he frequented. This man told him that a friend of his was selling his Apple IIe, which was only a year old and had absolutely every one of the features he wanted, and the guy was willing to accept a payment plan with a down payment of $500.

Wow! Fabulous! Great! We still didn't have the money. Stephen was disappointed, but not deterred. He said, "I'm getting my computer." He decided to call his father in Atlanta, Georgia and ask him for the down payment. I greeted this plan with a huge burst of laughter. His father didn't send money for child support.

What made him think he would send money for a computer? I kept this to myself, however.

I listened surreptitiously as Stephen asked his father for the money. I wasn't able to hear the response, but Stephen was extremely happy when he got off the telephone. His father was sending the money!

What?! And he did. I remember the day we picked up the computer and how Stephen set that computer up in exactly the same place he had been imagining the computer would be. I was so proud of my son and in awe of his mastery of spiritual principles.

Recently, I was talking to him about how he was my role model for faith and the power of imagination, and we talked about his getting the computer when the evidence clearly indicated that it was not possible. He told me, "I learned the principles from Sunday school, but I always knew the ability was there within me even before going to Unity. I just knew."

"Faith is the substance of things hoped for; the evidence of things not seen."[28]

I learned a lot from Stephen. Perhaps I should have been imagining getting the child support.

---

[28] Heb. 11:1, KJVA

In Deepak Chopra's *How to Know God*, the last chapter is about "Contacting God. It is about our Journey toward the Soul. In it, he says there are stages in our evolution toward the Soul, as there are stages to other aspects of our conscious evolution, and he lists seven stages of our journey toward Faith:[29]

1.   Faith is a matter of survival. If I don't pray to God, he can destroy me.

2.   I'm beginning to have faith in myself. I pray to God to help me get what I want.

3.   Faith brings me peace. I pray that life should be free from turmoil and distress.

4.   I have faith that inner knowledge will uphold me. I pray for more insight into God's ways.

5.   Faith tells me that God will support my every desire. I pray that I am worthy of his faith in me.

6.   Faith can move mountains. I pray to be God's instrument of transformation.

7.   Faith melts into universal being. When I pray, I find that I am praying to myself.

Myrtle Fillmore says ". . . *when we are full of faith and cooperate with this restoring principle of our being, God's work of restoration never ceases its activity in us"*.[30]

---

[29] Deepak Chopra, MD, *How to Know God*, (New York: Harmony Books 2000), p. 292-293.
[30] Myrtle Fillmore, *Myrtle Fillmore's Healing Letters,* (Missouri: Unity Books 1986), p. 58.

In *How to Let God Help You*, she says *"power belongs to [those] who know and when we are [totally] translated into the knowledge that the 'lower world is made after the pattern of the upper and inner world,' we will have power over all [the] appearances of sense".*[31]

In other words: all that God is we are, and the outer world is only a reflection of the inner world. This is certain. There is no uncertainty. This is Faith. It is something we can trust in, depend on and pray upon. Every miracle of Jesus was an exercise in Faith.

Does "Faith" require anything of us?

The Bible says: *Faith without works is dead.*[32]

A woman related to someone I once knew was a shining example of faith working in someone's life. She knew that everything she needed, required and desired would be provided for her; she would speak it and it would manifest. She had what appeared to be a perfect life—a great marriage, beautiful successful children, a job she was passionate about and many loving friends and relatives. One day, she received the news that her youngest child was killed in an accident. Within a year, her life was demolished. She grieved so hard she could not lay hold of her faith. Her marriage ended, she lost her job, her house and everything she owned and, finally, she gave up and died.

Faith does require that we do something—that we continue to hold the energy of faith high in the midst of our storms—to maintain the consciousness of faith that

---

[31] Myrtle Fillmore, *How to Let God Help You,* (Missouri: Unity Books 1986), p. 47.
[32] James 2:20

sustained us during the times when the sun was shining, in order to have it anchored in us when the rain is upon us.

A student in one of my classes argued that once we have faith, or the knowledge of it, we cannot turn it off or turn away from it. I agree and I disagree.

Just as we can accept and align with God's presence in our lives or reject it and refuse to align with God's presence in our lives, we can choose to align or not align with faith.

Although it is not the Truth that our faith is gone, it is a reality that we have disengaged our connection with the flow of it as an expression in our lives. We are very powerful and, when we are open channels to the flow of creative energy there is nothing we cannot create; however, the opposite is just as true. When we block the channels, either knowingly or unknowingly, that energy will not flow and manifestation will not take place.

I can see this in my own life. Almost two years ago I was diagnosed with glaucoma after having almost gone blind. I began to align with faith that my sight would be restored and I would drive again and once more read books as I so love to do. Although my vision has improved, it is still not improved enough to drive and it still takes great effort to read.

I am fully aware that, at some level, my faith is not yet equal to my desire and I have, therefore, not manifested restored vision. There is something yet for me to do or be in order to facilitate this transformation. It has not, however, tempted me to give up; in fact, it has only made me more determined to prove God.

All that is required of us is to hold fast to that faith even in the midst of the raging storm. Storms never stand still; they are always moving. If we can just find a tree of hope—even a branch—to hold onto until it has passed, the weather will clear up and the sun will shine upon us in all its glory.

Prayer works as a channel through which our Faith in God gives us the courage to walk through the storm without fear.

PAUSE FOR REFLECTION & STUDY

At this time I invite you to take some time to reflect on what you have read so far, if you wish, and allow these concepts to settle within your heart and your mind. If you are part of a Book Study Group, this may be a good time for discussion. Below are some Study Questions to assist you:

 What was the key ingredient in Stephen's process for manifestation of the computer that assured the outcome despite the appearance of what was possible?

 How do we know when to let go and surrender to God?

 What is the purpose of having faith?

 Should we pray for faith? Why? Why not?

The power of Jesus to heal was not in the particular words he used but was in the consciousness back of those words—the consciousness which knew their full significance and meaning.[33]

Ernest Holmes

What is the Role of Jesus Christ in Prayer?

Metaphysics teaches that invoking the name of Jesus Christ when you pray impresses upon your mind the Truth about yourself as a son/daughter of God with the potential for expressing that spiritual reality just as Jesus did.

Jesus perfectly exemplified what it is to be a spiritual offspring of God, expressing the activity of God for the good of the planet.

Jesus' role, then, is to be our constant exemplification of the "who" we are when we have established, in the manifest "Now," the relationship with God that was established in consciousness at the point of creation.

Jesus is our Way-shower, who stands above us pointing the way to our rightful place in the Kingdom of God that has been prepared for us in consciousness. By praying in His name, we open our consciousness to be led there by His guidance.

What Does it Mean to Pray "in the Name and Through the Power of Jesus Christ?"

And whatever you may ask in My name, that I will do, so that the Father may be glorified in the Son.
(John 14:13 MKJV)

---

[33] Ernest Holmes, *Good for You,* (California: Science of Mind Publications 1987), p.123.

First, let us look at some definitions that establish for us what "in the name and through the power of" mean:

Name:

A word or phrase that constitutes the distinctive designation of a person or thing.[34]

An arbitrary appellation received in the language of the intellect describing a mental image or thought picture. Name designates the "character" of a thing.[35]

In the Name of:

By authority of; for the reason of.[36]

The name of a great entity or person carries his/her name potency and whenever that name is repeated silently or audibly the attributes of that entity become manifest.[37]

Christ: The perfect idea of God in man.

Jesus: The perfect expression of the Divine Idea in man.

Jesus Christ: A union of the two—the idea and the expression; the perfect man demonstrated.

In the name and through the power of Jesus Christ is a powerful affirmation. Name designates the "character" of a thing. When we pray in the "name" of Jesus Christ, we are acknowledging those aspects of Jesus Christ within us

---

[34] Webster's Ninth New Collegiate Dictionary 1983

[35] Charles R. Fillmore, *The Revealing Word,* (Missouri: Unity Books 1959), p. 137.

[36] Webster's Ninth New Collegiate Dictionary 1983

[37] Charles R. Fillmore, *The Revealing Word,* (Missouri: Unity Books 1959), p. 138.

and in that moment we take on the Christ "character" or "nature" of Jesus.

It also means "by the authority of." So, when we say it, we are doing it according to the authority of the Christ or following the guidelines Jesus gave to his disciples during his ministry.

We are affirming that the creative activity of God that worked through Jesus works also through us.

There is power and authority in the name of Jesus Christ. We think of Christ as representing the power of God and Jesus as the activity of that power. We invoke the power that Jesus stood for when we pray in His name.

Jesus Christ represents power and authority in the realm of spiritual ideas. We are praying in the name of the greatest authority in the spiritual realm when we pray in the name of Jesus Christ.[38]

Jesus was the greatest proponent of the "I AM," and that is why when we exhort the power in the name of Jesus in affirmative prayer and meditation, there is a miraculous manifestation.

"When we ask in His name, it is with an earnest desire for that consciousness which Jesus possessed. When we ask in the name of Christ

Jesus we ask in the consciousness that in reality we are perfect children of the Father."[39]

---

[38] May Rowland, *The Magic of the Word*, (Missouri: Unity Books 1972) p. 134

[39] Charles R. Fillmore, *The Revealing Word*, (Missouri: Unity Books 1959), p. 112.

When we pray in the name and through the power of Jesus Christ, we tap into the Christ potential within us to support our prayer work for the realization of its highest possibility.

And, yet, there is absolutely no requirement that we pray *in the name and through the power of Jesus Christ.* As we have been remind throughout this book, we are one with our Creator (God, IAM, Source, Universe) and the point of connection is within us; therefore, we can pray in our own name for we are as close to God as Jesus was. Did he not say so?

Jesus' role in prayer is a powerful *reminder* of our own innate ability to manifest the Kingdom of God in the midst of the storm and upon planet earth NOW!

PAUSE FOR REFLECTION & STUDY

At this time I invite you to take some time to reflect on what you have read so far, if you wish, and allow these concepts to settle within your heart and your mind. If you are part of a Book Study Group, this may be a good time for discussion. Below are some Study Questions to assist you:

What was your early understanding of Jesus and prayer?

How did it make you feel? How do you feel about it now?

Do we have to believe in Jesus Christ in order to have our prayers answered?

What, if anything, has changed about your perception of Jesus?

The practice of meditation awakens you to the inner presence of God, putting you in touch with the divine desire to express through you limitlessly. Prayer enables you to carry God's desire for unlimited expression through your consciousness and into your body and external affairs.[40]

J. Douglas Bottorff

What is the Difference between Prayer and Meditation?

Meditation is the attuning of the mental body and physical body to its spiritual Source. Meditation is the stilling of the chaos that perpetually involves itself in our human existence and coming into a definitive point of reference where we meet as one with God. It is the "click" as the cylinders in the safe which has locked away our Truth, fall into place and open the door to our spiritual existence.

There are many forms of meditation, which are equally effective in creating desired results. The key is to find the path which rings true for us, individually, and to consistently practice until there is no longer any effort. It is not necessary to spend hours meditating. We can find ways of making meditation a part of our daily life with very little effort.

Meditation is a journey within. It is not just for monks and hermits or people who have a "calling." Jesus speaks of meditation throughout his teachings in the Bible and frequently went apart to commune with his Father in secret.

---

[40] J. Douglas Bottorf, *A Practical Guide to Meditation and Prayer,* (Missouri: Unity Books 1990), p.91.

Jack and Cornelia Addington assert that there is ". . . joy in the journey to meditation . . ." but sometimes it is ". . . easier to talk about the journey than to actually travel it."[41]

We make the journey and the destination difficult by "resistance." To quote the Borg in <u>Star Trek: The Next Generation</u>: "Resistance is Futile," because our soul yearns to return to the Source. The soul's deep hunger to return to its perfect existence is the cause of our restlessness. In our limited capacity while dwelling in the human experience, we perceive this yearning as the desire to acquire, striving for success, "movin' on up" (to a deluxe apartment in the sky); when, in Truth, it is nothing more or less than superconscious memory of origination—which is our ultimate destination.

So our subconscious self has created meditation to assist us in making the journey. It is like solving a riddle, putting together a jigsaw puzzle. As we meditate, the riddle becomes clear, the pieces of the puzzle fall into place.

In prayer, we speak to God (The Source) and make our desires known. In meditation, God/Source speaks to us and the path to our desires is revealed through the Silence.

In the midst of the storm, when we pray we call upon God to guide us; and when we meditate, we cease all struggles and await our Divine Guidance for a clear pathway out of the raging winds and the high waters.

---

[41] Jack and Cornelia Addington, *The Joy of Meditation* (Calif.: DeVORSS 1979), p. 8.

The Silence is a state of consciousness entered into for the purpose of putting man in touch with Divine Mind so that the soul may listen to the "still small voice.[42]

Charles Fillmore

What is the Silence?

Let's look, first, at how several metaphysicians answer that question:

> *"The Silence is a kind of stillness, a place of retreat into which we may enter and having entered, may know the Truth . . . In the silence, wisdom is given for every need."* [43]

> Charles Fillmore says the Silence is *"the highest form of prayer we know. The purpose of the Silence is to still the activity of personal thought so that the still small voice of God may be heard. In the Silence, Spirit speaks Truth to us and exactly that Truth we need at the moment."*[44]

> Gregg Braden, in *The Isaiah Effect*, says *"In [the] stillness, we allow creation to express itself through us in the moment."*[45]

> Deepak Chopra, in *How to Know God*, says *"Silence . . . is the mind's source."*[46]

> Frances Foulks, in *Effectual Prayer*, says *"[the] Silence is not inertia, not a drifting into something we know nothing about. Our bodies are relaxed but it is alive and ready to*

---

[42] Charles R. Fillmore, *The Revealing Word,* (Missouri: Unity Books 1959), p. 179

[43] Myrtle Fillmore, *How to Let God Help You,* (Missouri: Unity Books 1986), p. 87.

[44] Charles Fillmore, *Dynamics for Living,* (Missouri: Unity Books 1995), p. 98.

[45] Gregg Braden, *The Isaiah Effect,* (New York: Harmony Books 2000), p. 159.

[46] Deepak Chopra, *How to Know God,* (New York: Harmony Books 2000), p. 94.

act; our intellect is stilled, but it is alert and ready to be used."[47]

Asking in prayer only begins the work to bring our desires into manifestation. We must go into the Silence to receive the guidance of Spirit to put "feet" to our prayers. When we pray we talk to God, but in the Silence God talks to us.

There are two types of Silence:

Intellectual—limited in power, the silence where one's whole attention is fixed on the intellect where thought is the supreme power.

Spiritual—the constructive Silence where the attention is fixed on the heart and surrenders to Spirit.

The first step in Spiritual (or Scientific) Silence is to still the outer intellectual thoughts so that consciousness may become subservient to the Spirit within.[48]

Please be aware that this is not necessarily easy, however, simple it may appear, and takes consistent practice to make the shift from the outer activities and mind stuff in order to move into the Silence.

Douglas Bottorff, in *A Practical Guide to Meditation and Prayer*, says *"[the] biggest obstacle you will face in entering the silence through meditation is your own busy mind.*"[49]

---

[47] Frances Foulkes, *Effectual Prayer,* (Missouri: Unity Books 1979, 1986), p. 86.

[48] Charles and Cora Fillmore, *Teach Us to Pray,* (Missouri: Unity Books 1941),

[49] J. Douglas Bottorff, *A Practical Guide to Meditation and Prayer,* (Missouri: Unity Books 1990), p. 143.

When we have reached that place within where all the noises and confusion of the physical world have been turned off, we will know and experience our Creator at the deepest and most profound level possible.

We will also know, personally, what Jesus meant when he said "Father, glorify thou me with thine own self as thou didst glorify me before the world was."[50]

Exercise:

Take some time each day to practice the Silence:

1. Find a comfortable place where you won't be disturbed, and sit in a chair or on the floor in a position that won't cramp you or cause you to fidget.

2. Close your eyes and take three (or more) deep, cleansing breaths to relax you. Make sure your stomach fills up on the in-breath and flattens on the out—breath.

3. Let the Silence take you wherever it will. If any thoughts or images arise, take note of them and then release them. Try not to get caught up in what they are or what they mean . . . just let them go.

(When learning to do *Vipassana Meditation,* we are taught to think of our thoughts as boxcars on a freight train and simply observe them as they pass by without resistance. If, by chance, we mistakenly hop on one and

---

[50] John 17:5 KJVA

begin to ride, once we realize we're on the train, bring our focus back to the breath and return to the present moment. Resistance only causes our thoughts to fight harder to take control.)

4. Do this for five minutes. You may want to set an alarm clock or use a timer. As you become more accustomed to this practice, you may increase the time period.

5. If anything comes up for you, positive or negative, journal about it. The Silence is the process for receiving great insights as well as discovering some things that may be calling for healing.

Eventually you will feel that you have touched the presence of God. The purpose of the silence is to contact the Spirit within you. God is present within you. God is omnipresent, but you contact His presence at the center of your being. Say to yourself, "Be still." Relax. Practice being quiet. Relax. Let go. Feel the presence.[51]

The *Silence* is much more than the mere absence of noise. It is an experience—an activity of *Being*—and when we gain mastery over the brain and leave the outer where it belongs, we will not only connect with God but we will *know* God.

If we could maintain a daily practice of the Silence, it would provide us with great clarity in our lives and a

---

[51] May Rowland, *The Magic of the Word*, Unity Books, (Missouri), p. 153.

sense of what it feels like to stay calm and centered; and, when we are faced with turmoil and storms in our lives, we can tap into that feeling to bring us back to center.

PAUSE FOR REFLECTION & STUDY

At this time I invite you to take some time to reflect on what you have read so far, if you wish, and allow these concepts to settle within your heart and your mind. If you are part of a Book Study Group, this may be a good time for discussion. Below are some Study Questions to assist you:

- What is the difference between *prayer* and *meditation?*

- What is the purpose of meditation?

- Is it necessary to pray *and* meditate?

- If you are currently meditating, what impact, if any, does it have on your day or your life?

- What is your understanding of the Silence?

- Why should we allow time for the Silence?

Prayer involves more than a collection of words, thoughts, and intents.[52]
Rosemary Ellen Guiley

Is There More Than One Way to Pray?

There are many ways to pray, and many types of prayer; a few of which are: Invocation, Intercessory, Centering, Treatment, Chanting and Affirmative.

Invocation:

> *"The calling forth of the presence of Spirit through the power of the Word."* [53]

Prayer of Invocation: "Invoking the name of God (a deity, Jesus) is the greatest efficiency (expediter) of Prayer—Jesus always said 'Father'."[54]

Example: By repeating the name of God, I AM or Jesus, or by saying "Come Holy Spirit," we are offering a prayer of invocation.

Exercise:

Find a quiet place and a seat where you will be comfortable; close your eyes, take a few deep breaths and just say aloud "Come Holy Spirit" over and over until you begin to feel yourself relaxing and a quickening takes place in your body. Begin with a five-minute practice period and then increase

---

[52] Rosemary Ellen Guiley, *The Miracle of Prayer,* (New York: Pocket Books 1995), p. 89

[53] Charles R. Fillmore, *The Revealing Word,* (Missouri: Unity Books 1959), p. 109

[54] Emma Curtis Hopkins, *High Mysticism,* (Calif.: DeVorss & Co. No Year), p. 139

after a week or so until you are at approximately 15 minutes.

Intercessory Prayer:

"A prayer, petition or entreaty for another."[55]

In Intercessory Prayer, we intercede on behalf of another or pray to a Saint or other spiritual figure to intercede on our behalf or someone for whom we are praying.

Jesus frequently used Intercessory Prayers. In the 17th Chapter of John, you will find three examples of what is known as an Intercessory Prayer. Jesus first prayed for himself and then for all who would accept salvation through Him, when he said:

And now, Father, glorify thou me with thine own self with the glory I had with thee before the world was. I manifested thy name unto the men whom thou gavest me out of the world. (John 17:5,6)

I pray for them; I pray not for the world, but for those whom though has given me. (John 17:9)

Neither for these only do I pray, but for them also that believe on me. (John 17:20)

Example: The "Prayer of St. Francis" is an intercessory prayer.

Lord, make me an instrument of They peace.
Where there is hatred, let me sow love,
Where there is injury, pardon,
Where there is doubt, faith,
Where there is despair, hope,

---

[55] Webster's Ninth New Collegiate Dictionary, 1988 by Merriam-Webster.

Where there is darkness, light
Where there is sadness, joy.

O, Divine Master, grant that I may not so much seek
To be consoled as to console,
To be understood, as to understand,
To be loved, as to love.
For it is in giving that we receive,
It is in pardoning that we are pardoned,
It is in dying that we are born to eternal life.

Intercessory prayer is the primary type of prayer used by the Catholic Church. Their prayers are offered to the Virgin Mary or other Saints to intercede with God on their behalf.

Centering Prayer

Centering Prayer is actually a form of meditation or contemplation. Its purpose is to create conscious union with God. In it, we do not so much pray and reflect upon the innate condition of our oneness with that which created us. It is an ancient process, often traced back to monastic practices where one spends hours, days and even a lifetime aligning with and experiencing the presence of God.

The practice of Centering Prayer was the desired outcome of The Rosary in Catholicism. By meditating upon a desire or intention passionately as you touch each bead, you are moving away from the outer and toward the inner—taking the mind's natural tendency to wander aimlessly under control and keeping it focused on what is taking place in the moment.

Mind can be compared to an ocean, and momentary mental events such as happiness, irritation, fantasies and boredom to the waves that rise and fall upon its surface. Just as the waves can subside to reveal the stillness of the ocean's depth, so too is it possible to calm the turbulence of our mind to reveal its natural pristine clarity.[56]

The process, in itself, is very simple; however, the achievement is not easy but definitely possible. It takes consistent practice and a deep desire to know the feeling of God as reality to keep oneself on task. The key is loving intention.

Below is the process, as laid out by Basil Pennington, who is one of the leading teachers and proponents of the *Centering Prayer Method.*

Exercise:

1. Sit comfortably with your eyes closed, relax, and quiet yourself. Be in love and faith to God.

2. Choose a sacred word that best supports your sincere intention to be in the Lord's presence and open to His divine action within you (i.e. "Jesus", "Lord," "God," "Savior," "Abba," "Divine," "Shalom," "Spirit," "Love," etc.).

3. Let that word be gently present as your symbol of your sincere intention to be in the Lord's presence and open to His divine action within you. (Thomas Keating advises that the word remain unspoken.)

4. Whenever you become aware of anything (thoughts, feelings, perceptions, images, associations, etc.), simply return to your sacred word, your anchor.

---

[56] Kathleen MacDonald, *How to Meditate* (CITE)

Thomas Keating, another of the foremost authorities on *Centering Prayer,* says this method is not about concentrating on a sacred thought or focusing on one particular thing; it is about having our only goal be to establish the Will of God and maintain the experience of the presence of God.

In other words, as my most significant teacher of mysticism—Rev. Lafayette Seymour—says: God I want to know you more. And nothing else is necessary.

Prayer Treatment:

> A spiritual energy in the mental world, equipped with power and volition—as much power and volition as there is faith in it, given to it by the mind of the one using it—and, operating through the Law of Cause and Effect, knows exactly how to work and what methods to use and just how to use them.[57]

> Spiritual realization of God's Truth for oneself or another; a prayer of faith and understanding for healing, harmony, wisdom, prosperity or any other good that man may desire, the object of which is to raise the consciousness of the one being treated to a high spiritual consciousness by which healing is accomplished. [58]

A Prayer Treatment is for the purpose of inducing an inner realization of perfection in the mentality of the one praying. That inner realization, acting through Mind, operates through the one being Treated. The word, operating through Mind, sets the Law in motion.

---

[57] Ernest Holmes, *The Science of Mind,* (New York: Tarcher/Putnam 1938, 1998), p. 58

[58] Charles R. Fillmore, *The Revealing Word,* (Missouri: Unity Books 1959), p. 198

It is a conscious movement of thought and the work begins and ends in the thought of the one giving the Treatment.

We do not put the power *into* the words; rather, we allow the power of the Law to flow *through* the words, and the one who most completely believes in this power will produce the best results.

Giving a treatment without believing that Divine Order is the natural outcome creates a negative treatment. The degree to which the Treatment works is solely based upon the degree to which we *believe* it will work.

Ernest Holmes says if we doubt our ability to give an effective Treatment, we should Treat ourselves to remove all doubts.

For example, you may say: *I am convinced that this word has power and I firmly believe in it. I trust it to produce the right results in my life (or the life of the one for whom you are using your word).*

We must work Treatments with *Expectancy* through conscious recognition and receptivity. Accept, believe and leave everything to the Law, and there is no reason to mention the challenge or difficulty when treating

"There are two methods of *Treatment*:

- *Argumentative*—*a process of mental reasoning in which the practitioner argues to himself about his patient; presenting a logical argument to Universal Mind (or Principle). If it carries with it complete evidence in favor of the patient, he/ she should be healed.*

- *Realization*—*a method by which the practitioner realizes within him/herself the perfect state of the patient; a purely spiritual and meditative process of contemplating the perfect expression through the human man or woman."* [59]

Examples: Treating for an illness (someone has cancer):

<u>Argumentative</u>

The word I now speak is for Karen Davidson. She is a perfect and complete manifestation of Pure Spirit and Pure Spirit cannot be diseased; consequently, Karen is not diseased.

<u>Realization</u>

The word I now speak is for Karen Davidson. (Then realize the ONLY Perfect Presence.) God is all there is; there is nothing else. God is in Karen Davidson, she is now a perfect being, she is now a spiritual being.

"Either method works and produces the same results. One is a logical argument in the mind of the Practitioners to convince themselves of the Truth of Being. The other is the instant cutting through of all appearances to the Reality behind all things." [60]

Holmes says, "when we can pursue only the [method] of *pure realization*, we will have attained the ideal method." [61]

The *Argumentative* is made up of affirmations and denials. The *realization* method is the most powerful; however, we can see that there is also great power in the *argumentative* method.

Following a Treatment comes *Demonstration*.

[59] Ernest Holmes, *The Science of Mind,* (New York: Tarcher/Putnam 1938, 1998), p. 170-174

[60] Ernest Holmes, *The Science of Mind,* (New York: Tarcher/Putnam 1938, 1998), p. 173

[61] Ibid. 173

A Demonstration is made when the thing is accomplished that the one treating desires to achieve. It is answered Prayer. When word takes form, that is a *Demonstration*. [62]

Charles Fillmore defines *Demonstration* as "The proving of a Truth principle in one's body or affairs; manifestation of an ideal brought about by one's conformity in thought, word and act to the creative Principle of God."

He says, "[It] is a metaphysical law that there are three steps in every demonstration: the recognition of Truth as it is in Principle; holding an idea; and acknowledging fulfillment. 'Whatsoever ye shall ask in prayer, believing, ye shall receive.' (Matthew 21:22)." [63]

Fillmore further states, "Truth must be demonstrated. It defines itself." [64]

---

[62] Ibid., p. 174-175

[63] Charles R. Fillmore, *The Revealing Word,* (Missouri: Unity Books 1959), p. 52

[64] Charles Fillmore, *Dynamics For Living,* (Missouri: Unity Books 1959, 1994), p. 109.

<u>Chanting</u>:

Chanting is a form of meditative prayer, in which a Mantra is used to still the mind and withdraw from the intellectual focus on the outer to the spiritual intention of the inner. Chanting uses sound vibrations as a form of expression for inner discovery through meditation.

A Mantra is a word, phrase, hymn or chant used to still the mind and make it totally receptive to the Divine Consciousness.

One of the most well-known and powerful mantras is *OM* or *AUM*. It originated with the Hindu religion and is also used by Buddhists and others. It is considered to be the universal vibration. It translates to "I Am."

> Dr. David Fontana says, "there is no doubt that the prolonged repetition of certain sounds—especially rhythmical sounds—can influence the physical rhythm of the brain in a way [that] assists the meditator in achieving the relaxed yet focused concentration that meditation demands."[65]

---

[65] David Fontana, Ph.D., *The Meditator's Handbook,* (Mass.: Element 1992), p. 99.

Exercise:

Close your eyes and say the Om (pronounced ah-oohm) for one minute. Notice how you feel and what the energy around you feels like.

From 1981 until 1996, I was actively involved in the Siddha Yoga practice and community. Curumay is still my Guru. I spent so many hours chanting during that time period that, to this day, the mantra *om namah shivaya* still takes me into that altered state of calm and bliss.

Affirmative Prayer

This type of prayer and *Treatment* are most accurately aligned with the concepts of the science of prayer that we have been discussing throughout this book.

Affirmative prayer is a form of prayer or a metaphysical technique that is focused on a positive outcome rather than a negative situation

www.wikipedia.org

What is Affirmative Prayer?

Affirmative Prayer is a Prayer of assurance, acknowledging that God has already supplied our every need; accepting the blessing and giving thanks before it is apparent to the human eye; declaring that God stands ever-ready to provide for us.

With Affirmative Prayer, there is no need to beg or beseech God to fulfill our requests, because all that we could possibly require has already been provided for us. It is already manifest in the invisible realm and awaits our calling it forth into the visible. It actually transforms particles of energy into substance or matter. We will discuss this more in the Chapter on Quantum Prayer.

Affirmative Prayer is the prayer method used by Jesus, who always prayed knowing in advance that his request would be granted.

It accepts what has already been provided and gives thanks in advance of its visible manifestation. You might say it is a confirmation of something agreed upon between us and God—like a Letter of Agreement.

Affirmative Prayer uses the combined concepts of *Denials* and *Affirmations*.

Denials

Denials are a mental process by which we erase from our consciousness any false beliefs that are contrary to the Truth of our Being. Denial clears away belief in anything that is not of God and makes room for confirming Truth.

Are we denying that a condition exists? What are we denying?

We are not denying that a particular situation or condition exists or that we are experiencing it right now; however, we *are* denying that it has any power over us. We are denying that it can prevent us from manifesting our good.

EXAMPLE: I deny that the appearance of my bank account in any way reflects the abundant good that is mine by divine birthright.

Affirmations

Affirmations are the "yes" action of the mind; the act of affirming or declaring the Truth; the mental movement that confidently and persistently emphasizes the Truth of Being in the face of all appearances to the contrary.

Affirmations are statements of the Truth about God, the Truth about us and the Truth about our relationship with God.

What are we affirming?

We are affirming that we know as fact we deserve our good, and that it will be manifested accordingly.

EXAMPLE: I am the prosperous child of a wealthy and loving Parent whose good pleasure is to give me the Kingdom of Heaven right here and right now.

When we use *Denials* and *Affirmations* in our Affirmative Prayers, we activate the scientific process of prayer and assure right action through the Law of Mind-Action, which produces right outcome.

Deny, first, the appearance before you and then affirm the invisible Truth.

> *The Power within me is greater than that which is before me.*

Remember, *faith is the substance of things hoped for; the evidence of things not seen.* (Heb. 11:1)

Affirmations affirm the faith you have in God's willingness to pour you out a blessing even before there is even a glimpse of it.

Affirm it!

Believe it!

See it!

In her book, *Handbook of Positive Prayer*, Hypatia Hasbrouck provides us with a two pronged method for composing our own affirmations:

1. "Begin any prayer statement with either 'I know that,' 'I affirm that' or 'I give thanks that (or for).'

2. Use the present tense forms throughout the prayer, and whenever possible insert the word *now*."[66]

Exercise:

Take a current challenge in your life and create a *Denial* and an *Affirmation* about it. Use them seven times a day for 7 days. After that, let the energy rest and begin to bring forth your good.

May Rowland says, "In Unity we emphasize the prayer of decree or agreement; however, the affirmative prayer is not unique with us. Jesus used the affirmative prayer. Isaiah and many of the other prophets of the Old Testament used affirmative prayer. For example,

David prayed: 'Mine eyes are ever toward Jehovah; for he will pluck my feet out of the net.'

Isaiah prayed: 'Behold, God is my salvation; I will trust, and will not be afraid, for Jehovah is my strength and song; he is my salvation.'" [67]

Notice that David said <u>will</u> not *might* or *if I am good*. There is not one shred of doubt in that affirmative prayer. It is clear that he believes, no, *knows* his prayer will be answered.

Isaiah totally trusted that God would be the strength on which he could stand and would deliver.

Many affirmative prayers begin with the "I AM" Statement. For example: "I AM one with the ever present, overflowing

---

[66] Hypatia Hasbrouck, *Handbook of Positive Prayer,* (Missouri: Unity Books 1984), p. 49

[67] May Rowland, *Dare to Believe*, (Missouri: Unity Books, 1961), pp. 190-191.

and unlimited substance of God. I AM blessed with all that I need, require and desire to live a joy-filled and abundant life. I trust in the powerful outworking of God in this situation and in the circumstances of my life now."

In other words, affirm your good and it <u>will</u> appear.

Gratitude always follows *Affirmative Prayer*. Because we are firm in our faith that our good will manifest, we offer gratitude for it before it out-pictures in our lives.

Exercise:

> Take one current challenge in your life. Create an Affirmative Prayer, being sure to add to it a statement of gratitude.

Example: If your current challenge is finances, you might pray:

> I AM the prosperous beloved child of God and all the power of the universe gathers together to fulfill my every need. I AM truly grateful for all of the miraculous ways in which God brings unlimited prosperity into my life now. Thank you God for the good that is mine right now. Amen

Pray your Affirmative Prayer, consistently, for twenty-one (21) days and then put it away. Allow the seeds you have sown to germinate. Begin noticing as they sprout and then bloom in your life.

Don't be tempted to go check on it. You have surrendered it to GOD and it is being done in divine timing. If you feel there is a part you must play in the manifestation, pray and ask for guidance so you are following the direction of the

Holy Spirit and not your ego's need to fix it because you feel you need to be *doing* something. Do-be-do-be-do is a song for Frank Sinatra. Your new song is Be-do-be-do-be. Let go, let God and just BE.

Many times, when the storm comes, we are just too emotionally caught up in it to think about how to pray. At those times, if we can just say "God help me" it will bring us back to our center and we can affirm God's goodness and the perfect outcome.

In the beginning was the word and the word was with God and the word was God.

(John 1:1)

What's the Word?

For a very long time, I really thought I understood what John 1:1 meant, until I discovered Neville Goddard's book *Your Faith is Your Fortune.* I was preparing a Sunday message of the same title and was filling in for Rev. Kevin Ross at Christ Unity Church, who was developing a series based on the book. Due to a prior engagement, he invited me to begin the series. And what a blessing that was!

Neville, as he is affectionately called by all of us devoted readers and ascribers to his theories and insights, had been one of my favorite authors for 25 years since being introduced by Rev. Lafayette Seymour at Unity Center of Truth in the Nation's Capitol; however, I had not previously connected with this particular book.

In the very first chapter of *Before Abraham Was,* he sets the stage for every conceivable approach to manifesting from *Substance* into *Reality.* On this subject he quotes from John.

Here is the scripture in its entirety:

In the beginning was the Word, and the Word was with God, and the Word was God. He was in the beginning with God. All things came into being through Him and without Him not even one thing came into being that has come into being. (John 1:1-3)

And Neville's take on it is that,

"In the beginning was the unconditioned awareness of being, and the unconditioned awareness of being became conditioned by imagining itself to be something, and the unconditioned awareness of being became that which it had imagined itself to be; so did creation begin."[68]

If your mouth is hanging open and you are not yet able to speak, join the club. This literally blew my mind; however, after reading the entire chapter and pursuing some basic definitions, this masterfully-framed concept began to unveil itself to me and I knew it was something that could open our minds more expansively to the *Power of the Word.*

What, then, is he saying here and what does it teach us about the *Word?*

If something is *unconditioned,* we can say "it is neither shaped, formed nor yet defined". It has not yet *assimilated.* It is, theoretically, like the Quantum Field where energy continually exists as Particles (potential/possibility) until some outside force causes it to be *conditioned* into a Wave.

We know that *awareness* is simply consciousness or that to which we have been awakened. For example, when we become aware of a sound outside of our window, we actually hear it; however, until our attention became focused upon it in one way or another, we may be oblivious to it or it may simply exist for us as *white noise.*

Neville, in his brilliance, is saying that all things come forth into manifestation from the endless, formless, no-thingness

---

[68] Neville Goddard, *Your Faith is Your Fortune* (CA: G&J Publishing Co., 1941), p. 4.

of the principle of first conceiving of something (imagining it, having the idea of it), then becoming that which one conceives (feeling it, having faith in it), followed by the manifestation (expression, having it evolve into reality) of that which was first involved, ideated or conceived.

What is this *nothingness*?

God is all and God is nothing—God is nothing or no-thing as the unseen. God is all from the perspective of that which is made manifest.

It is the I AM. It is the Law of Being . . .

Being is existence; that which is. The Law of Being says that *our outer conditions or circumstances are at all times aligned with our inner state of being*. Our "inner state of being" is also known as our consciousness. Another way of saying it is *as within, so without.*

We become that which we are aware of being. Simply stated: You are who you believe you are; subsequently, what you call into being as the outer conditions of your life match who you believe you are (or are worthy of) at the deepest level of your being, your existence, your consciousness.

Nietzsche said "if a man quacks like a duck and walks like a duck, then who's to say that he isn't a duck?"

I would go further: Who's to say that he didn't actually make himself a duck?

How does this relate to *The Power of the Word?*

The term itself comes from the Greek word *Logos* and means *the divine archetype idea that contains all ideas, the Son of God, spiritual man in manifestation. Divine Mind in action. The Word of God; creative power, Christ consciousness formulated by universal Principle.*

The activity by which God reveals Himself; the thought of God or the sum total of God's creative power.[69]

The Word gives order and regularity to the movement of things, and is the divine dynamic, the energy and self-revelation of God.

So, the *Word* is the "unconditioned awareness" Neville is referring to in his interpretation of John 1:1 and is clearly in alignment with Charles Fillmore's definition of *Word.*

This, then, leads us to presume that when our words are spoken they align energetically with that endless, formless, unconditioned awareness and draws forth from it that which is *intentioned* by our consciousness and becomes the *conditions* we experience in our physical domain.

Additionally, the *Law of Being* forms it by the idea we have of who we are: worthy/unworthy; child of God/miserable sinner.

We are co-creating with God (the Grand Operational Design) regardless of the outcome or manifestation of our words because God is willing to give us even those things that are not necessarily good for us through the freedom of our *Will.*

---

[69] Charles Fillmore, *The Revealing Word* (MO: Unity Books, 1959)

This substantiates the statement in our chapter *What is Beyond Prayer?* That "all prayer is answered."

In the Bible, it often refers to the "two-edged sword." This symbolizes the Word. The Word has such power that it cuts two ways: positive and negative. How we choose to use it determines the effect it has upon our lives and us.

Charles Fillmore, in *Christian Healing*, says "As an example of the vibratory power of the spoken word, a vocalist can shatter a wineglass by concentrating upon it certain tones. Every time we speak we cause the atoms of the body to tremble and change their places. Not only do we cause the atoms of our own body to change their position, but we raise or lower the rate of vibration and otherwise affect the bodies of others with whom we come in contact."[70]

One of my favorite songs of the 60s was Cameo's *Word Up!* In it, they say "what's the word? Word up!"

It tells me that our words should always be sent forth from the *upper* level of our consciousness, as the Universe is already always listening and will rise up to the level of our words.

When I was a little girl, there was a little exchange the very hip people would have when they met each other on the street. It went like this:

Person 1: What's the Word?
Person 2: Thunderbird.
Person 1: What's the price?
Person 2: Thirty twice.

---

[70] Fillmore, *Christian Healing* (MO: Unity Books, 19__) p. 65.

I have absolutely no idea what they were talking about. I do know that there was a cheap wine called "Thunderbird" and that the price of it was somewhere around 60 cents or so, but since we're looking at the message in *The Word* could there be a message for us in this exchange?

Maybe Person 1 was actually asking "What are you aware of? Oh well, that might be a stretch but I thought it would be fun to include it. It may just trigger an amusing memory.

What's the Word? Good, all good, nothing but good.

Carefully consider the words you use and the thoughts you think, but be gentle with yourself when you misuse the Word. Just erase the previous statement or thought, forgive yourself and replace it with a higher vibration word.

In other words, "Word Up!" Say it with me: "Word up! Word up! Word up!

You really need to spend time, at least twenty minutes, in total quiet and stillness. You need to become totally at one not only with the space of love and healing within you but also without you.[71]

Rosemary Ellen Guiley

How Do We Prepare Ourselves for Prayer?

If we are to have the results we desire, we must mentally and spiritually prepare ourselves for prayer.

Prayer is an experience. Prayer is more than the words that we speak when we are trying to get our point across to God; so, we must prepare ourselves in order to have the fullest possible experience and the maximum result.

Unity Institute teaches that there are Seven Necessary Conditions for Effective Prayer:

1. God should be recognized as Source.

   Turn within and come to the realization that there is only one Source of all our good—God.

2. Oneness with God should be acknowledged

   Know that we are one with God (Source) and all that God is and has is ours.

3. Prayer must be made within the secret place.

   Seek the connection with Spirit in the deepest regions of our being—go within that place in consciousness where we find the portal to this experience.

4. The door must be closed on all thoughts and interest of the outer world.

---

[71] Rosemary Ellen Guiley, *The Miracle of Prayer,* (New York: Pocket Books 1995), p. 89.

Let go of the cares and concerns of everyday circumstances and surrender in total communion with God. Let go of all the laundry lists we constantly have running in our minds.

5. It must be believed that the answer/manifestation has already been received.

   Know, as Jesus knew, that we already have everything; it is merely waiting to be recognized by us. Trust.

6. The Kingdom of God must be desired above all things and be sought first.

   Regardless of the need or concern, we must desire to know God more. By knowing God more, we come to the realization that the Kingdom is already ours.

7. The mind must let go of every unforgiving thought.

   We must forgive absolutely everyone, especially ourselves, before we approach the altar of God.

(Notes in *italics* added by Author.)

To establish these conditions, we must prepare our minds to align with Principle, and scripture provides us with excellent support for this process:

1. **Forgive:** *So if you are offering your gift at the altar and there remember that your brother has any grievance against you, leave your gift at the altar and go. First make peace with your brother, and then come back and present your gift.* (Matthew 5:23 RSV)

2. **Reconcile:** (your desire—know what you really want) *Therefore I say unto you, whatsoever things ye desire, when ye pray, believe that ye receive them, and ye shall have them.* (Mark 11:24 KJVA)

3. **Be in integrity:** *He that followeth after righteousness and mercy findeth life, righteousness, and honor.* (Prov. 21:21 KJVA)

4. **Align:** *But if I do, though ye believe me not, believe the works: that ye may know, and believe, that the Father is in me, and I in him.* (John 10:38 KJVA)

5. **Feel it:** *And now, O Father, glorify thou me with thine own self with the glory which I had with thee before the world was.* (John 17:5 KJVA)

6. **Believe/Have Faith:** *And Jesus answering said unto them, have faith in God. For verily I say unto you, That whosoever shall say unto this mountain, Be thou removed, and be thou cast into the sea; and shall not doubt in his heart, but shall believe that those things which he saith shall come to pass; he shall have whatsoever he saith.* (Mark 11:22 KJVA) [Note: The original language translated to "the faith of God."]

Exercise:

For seven days, let go of your normal methods of prayer and pray only this: "God, I want to know You more."

Pray this in the morning before you get out of bed, while you are getting dressed, on your way to work or to take the kids to school, during the day when "stuff" happens, on your way home in the midst of bumper-to-bumper traffic, and at night before you close your eyes.

In praying "God, I want to know You More," you are putting God first in everything. When you put God first, you are seeking the source of all that is and when that relationship is established, everything else will follow.

Jesus said, *But seek ye first the kingdom of God, and his righteousness; and all these things shall be added unto you.* (Mat 6:33)

The word *seek* comes from the Greek and Hebrew words meaning "to worship."

Kingdom comes from the Greek word meaning "royalty" or "to rule."

Righteousness is from the Greek word meaning "equity." Metaphysically, it means "right-thinking."

Finally, the word *added* is from the Greek and Hebrew words meaning "place additionally, annex, and repeat."

When we pray "God, I want to know You More," we are "seeking first the Kingdom of God." We are worshiping the Source of our supply first. We are seeking the authority and the equity of God, so that all our good—not merely that which we need at the time—is placed additionally into every aspect of our lives.

Rather than believing that our jobs, paychecks, savings accounts, investments and other ways are the source of our supply, we have shifted our thinking in the right direction and are turning to the One Source.

God is the *means* and all the others are the *ways* through our good is expressed in the visible realm.

As we actively engage in this exercise it trains us to look only to God for everything, because that Source will never fail us. When the storms of life are raging, it is easier for us to turn to God rather than our fears.

PAUSE FOR REFLECTION & STUDY

At this time I invite you to take some time to reflect on what you have read so far, if you wish, and allow these concepts to settle within your heart and your mind. If you are part of a Book Study Group, this may be a good time for discussion. Below are some Study Questions to assist you:

 What is *Affirmative Prayer?* How does it differ from other types of prayer?

 Does positive prayer always bring positive results?

 Is a *denial* a form of evasion? Does it mean that a condition does not exist?

 Why is it so important to follow a *denial* with an *affirmation*?

 Why is it difficult to enter into the silence? What would help?

 Why is it necessary to set aside a definite prayer time and select a quiet place in which to pray or meditate?

 What prayer method(s) have you used in the past? How does it differ from the method you are currently using or plan to use?

While your offering is still before the altar, first go and make peace with your brother, then come and make your offering.

(Mat 5:24 BBE)

Why Is It Helpful to Forgive *Before* we Pray?

Of all the processes for spiritual healing that we learn in our quest to be free from pain and suffering, forgiveness is the most difficult and the most rewarding. If we can grasp the true meaning of forgiveness and its power, we are propelled light years into higher consciousness.

To forgive, metaphysically, means *to give for*; to give up the false for the true.

To "reconcile" with our brother means to forgive anything we have against anyone.

What Jesus is saying in Matthew 5:24 is that, if we are holding any unforgiveness toward ourselves or anyone, we cannot get to our highest good (the altar).

Forgiveness erases error from both mind and body, simultaneously. It is only through forgiveness that true spiritual healing can occur. We must forgive thought, word or deed that bears harm from ourselves to others and from others to us. We must forgive absolutely everyone, without exception.

True forgiveness is based on the premise that only love is real, anything else is a misperception and, therefore, an illusion. If this is true, then what we perceive as attack or aberrant behavior is merely looking through the eyes of the ego and not the heart. If only love is real, the attack or behavior never really occurred. What we failed to see was our brother's or sister's cry for love; what we failed to do was give it.

This does not mean that those persons who kill, maim, hurt and destroy others do not need to be taken out of the mainstream of society and given an opportunity to heal in a place where they can do no further harm. What it does mean, however, is that we must forgive them and see their innocence in spite of their behavior.

When we forgive, we are not accepting harmful or destructive behavior but we are recognizing the Innocence that is the Truth at the core of all creation, and offering that transformed perception as our gift to release both of us in the Holy Instant.

> *In the Holy instant the condition of love is met, for minds are joined without the body's interference, and where there is communication there is peace.* [72]

Exercise:

Make a list of everyone you have harmed in any way, whether they know about it or not. Then make a list of everyone who has harmed you in any way, whether they know about it or not. Go back as far in time as possible. If there is any unforgiveness toward your parents or caregivers, put them on your list as well. This process may take you several hours or several days, depending upon how difficult you decide this is. Once you are satisfied with your list, take each name one-by-one

---

[72] *A Course in Miracles,* (CA: Fdn. For Inner Peace 1975, 1985, 1992), T14 . . . XI.7:1, p. 328.

and do the following exercise as if they were there in front of you and you were looking deeply into their eyes, saying:

I give you to the Holy Spirit as part of myself. I know that you will be released, unless I want to use you to imprison myself. In the name of my freedom I choose your release, because I recognize that we will be released together. [73]

In the nine years since the first release of this book, I have discovered the most powerful process for releasing, letting go and healing the old hurts is Radical Forgiveness©, the work of Colin Tipping.

Radical Forgiveness© is a step-by-step process that uses energetic tools to forgive at a cellular level. It's simple, works at the level of the heart and you don't even have to believe in it to achieve a result. All that is required of you is to do it!

If you would like to know more about this process and its tools, visit Colin's website www.radicalforgiveness.com or my website www.spiritawakened.com.

It will transform your life in ways you never imagined and free you from even the bondages you were not aware of. Colin says, *forgiveness is no longer an option, it is our destiny.*[74]

---

[73] *A Course in Miracles,* (CA: Fdn. For Inner Peace 1975, 1985, 1992), T14 . . . XI.7:1, p. 329.

[74] Colin Tipping, Radical Forgiveness (CO: Sounds True, Inc. 2009)

Unforgiveness keeps us in bondage to the people or situations we are unable or unwilling to forgive. In order to release ourselves, we must release others. Forgiveness is the key that unlocks the door and releases us, so that we may release others.

Enlightenment for a wave is the moment the wave realizes that it is water.
At that moment, all fear of death disappears.

Thich Nhat Hanh

What is beyond Prayer?
Quantum Prayer: A Leap into the Unknown

There are vibrations in space that our men of science have not yet discerned or measured. These undiscovered quantities are related to the Mind of Being and must be apprehended through the unfolding in man of supermind faculties. When the trained Christian metaphysician prays, he can with a disciplined consciousness, make contact with these forces in the ether and through them gain a certain unity with the Mind of Being. The consciousness thus attained is usually designated as the Christ consciousness or the mind of the Lord Jesus Christ. When that union is attained an increase in spiritual power is felt and one has the assurance of the activity of spiritual principles within, of which one has had hitherto no awareness.[75]

Charles Fillmore knew, even in 1959, that something was up: that there was more to this mind, this body, this Universe, than that of which we were aware. As he was fascinated by science, he consistently kept abreast of the most cutting-edge scientific research as a result of his deeply-affirmed belief that science and religion were in a relationship. You can see this, particularly, in his book *Atom-Smashing Power of Mind*.

By the time the movie, *What the Bleep* hit the theater screen the masses were ready for this Truth and it certainly sparked a passion for Quantum Physics within me. As I explored this relatively new science, it began to creep into

---

[75] Charles & Cora Fillmore, *Teach Us to Pray*, (Missouri: Unity Books 1959), p. 43

my classes, workshops and writings; thus, was born the 2006 workshop and now this chapter: Quantum Prayer.

What do I mean by Quantum Prayer?"

Quantum

1. A discrete quantity of energy proportional in magnitude to the frequency of the radiation it represents;

2. An analogous discrete amount of any other physical quantity, such as momentum or electric charge

The word *quantum* refers to an inordinate or immeasurable amount or degree of something, as reflected in the definition above, and this chapter is an exploration into what is *beyond* that which we have discussed throughout the rest of the book. It implies and sets out to show the modern-day scientific premise undergirding prayer and theories that provide proof that it works. It also delves into what is *beyond* prayer itself.

Quantum Prayer, based on the above premises, would be prayer at its highest possibility calling forth from the immeasurable that which can be measured in its manifest state.

For well over 100 years, the theologies of Unity and Religious Science have been merging, teaching and proving the power of understanding the principles of energy behind Prayer. For most of that time, it has drawn a small and select group of followers of these doctrines; however, through movies, television shows, books, song lyrics and social media, it is now almost commonplace and more and more a part of the consciousness and conversation of the masses.

Because this book subscribes to providing the reader with all the information they require in learning how to pray and have prayer work in their lives, it seemed important to add something about how Quantum Physics holds profound implications and discoveries that provide greater insight into what prayer is and how it evolves from a desire to an actual manifestation.

So, where do we begin? Perhaps a look at what we know about prayer and what we don't know about prayer helps establish a foundation from which to build a premise for what is *beyond* prayer.

What do you already know about prayer?

Take some time to write what you have discovered so far both from this book and your own life experience. You may use this space or a separate sheet of paper.

_____

_____

_____

_____

_____

_____

_____

_____

What you may <u>not</u> know about Prayer . . .

* Absolutely <u>all</u> prayer is answered.

   This Foundation Premise is that: We are Spiritual Beings, living in a Spiritual Universe, governed by Spiritual Laws. (You may substitute the word "energy" instead of "spiritual" if it is more comfortable for you. It still means the same thing.)

- Prayer has very little to do with the spoken word.

- Prayer is not really about <u>what</u> you are praying for.

- Prayer is, in large part, based on *Intention.*

- Prayer is based on scientific laws and is provable.

- What means more than anything else, when praying, is whether we believe (or not) and *what* we believe.

The very first premise is enough in itself to justify acquiring knowledge of the scientific principles that govern the practice of prayer and its results—the reason being that in our reality, it appears that "all prayer is <u>not</u> answered." Perhaps looking at the root meaning of the word will help.

The word "Prayer" comes from the Aramaic word *Sloth* and means *to set a trap; to make an adjustment.*

So what does that actually mean?

To set a trap: Prayer is an activity that prepares the mind to capture insights into the attributes, characteristics, ideas and the processes of that which we call Power, Source or Presence toward which we direct our prayers.

To make an adjustment: Prayer is the activity of adjusting our minds, in every situation, to the higher spiritual standard unfolding in us as a direct result of our inner growth and development.

As we discussed, in the chapter on *How Does Prayer Work?,* prayer is an energy vibration that is a composite of thoughts, feelings and emotions and is thrust out into the universal realm of energy (The Quantum Field) by desire, intention and faith. Like the subatomic particles that began to gravitate toward each other at the onset of the creation of the universe, the energy signature of our prayers gravitates toward other energy signatures that resonate at the same rate of frequency and begin to form patterns that facilitate a universe that returns to us as our experience.

Quantum Physics helps us understand the inner workings of prayer and removes much of the mystery that surrounds prayer.

What is Quantum Mechanics?

Quantum Mechanics is another name for Quantum Physics, a relatively new branch of science first introduced by Niels Bohr and Max Planck and later expanded upon by Albert Einstein, which is the study of matter and energy.at the deepest and most subtle levels possible.

It is the Physics of *possibilities*. It states and proves that atoms are actually possibilities awaiting focus, intention or choice. It further indicates that every one of us affects the Quantum Field (or field of energy) in several ways: words, thoughts, emotions and even movement. Not only do we affect this energy but we are part of this energy.

I won't go into this in any more detail. I am simply giving you enough information to help you understand that there is an actual science to how our prayers work. I recommend further exploration on your own. A great beginning for the novice is the movie *What the Bleep do We Know?*

It is enough right now to simply say everything is energy and prayer is energy; that when we pray, we are participating in the process of transferring atoms from possibility to reality.

When you are <u>not</u> looking, this energy exists as particles of possibility; when you <u>are</u> looking, they are waves of experience—potential strips of reality until we choose. Additionally, these particles are alive and vibrating, sending out a signal or energy pattern.

EXAMPLE: The realm of Energy is like a tremendous banquet, with tables and tables of food available for you to eat.

When you are not looking at the food, it simply exists there as items for possible consumption and enjoyment if anyone happen upon it. It is cooked, arranged upon platters or in chafing dishes and emitting delightfully tempting smells that fill the air.

When you are looking at the food, the experience begins as your senses take over. Your nose begins to take in all the different aromas and your taste buds begin to imagine the potential flavors and textures of the food. It is as if the good is calling to us to come and partake of it.

It is still not yet a reality until we choose the food we wish to sample and then take our first bite, bringing into all of our senses the actual experience of the food. That, then, is possibility expressed or actualized as reality.

Energy/Atoms are not things—only possibilities or potential. That which we call God is actually Energy or Infinite Possibility-Infinite Potential.

Prayer, then, is the action that calls forth the possibility of the expression of energy into our lives to create the reality we desire.

Once we have prayed, we have filled our plate with food and are moving toward the table to sit down and eat.

5 Types of Prayer Energy

There are five (5) types of Prayer Energy: 1. Conscious; 2. Unconscious; 3. Positive; 4. Negative; and 5. Miraculous.

Conscious Prayer is one of the most common types of prayer. During conscious prayer, the conscious mind conceives of a need and directs energy toward a source of higher aid and support

Unconscious is probably the most common type of prayer. During unconscious prayer, the unconscious mind takes over the process of prayer, without the aid of the conscious mind, and directs the energy for its own purposes. This happens without the knowledge or awareness of the individual.

Positive uses the positive aspects of the divine creative force in order to bring about a desired positive outcome. Positive prayer is directed by positive thoughts and feelings. In Unity, we also refer to this type of prayer as "Affirmative Prayer".

Negative uses the negative aspects of the divine creative force in order to bring about a desired negative outcome. Negative prayer is directed by negative thoughts and feelings.

Miraculous uses the force of the miraculous to bring about a desired result. This type of prayer generally embodies the use of a specific tool or object to empower the energy of the prayer beyond that which the human mind is capable of generating.

These types of energy pulsating in and through our prayers, whether consciously or unconsciously, manipulate the particles within the Quantum Field and begin a movement toward us as a wave. When we work to stay in the present moment and be aware of our words, thoughts, feelings emotions and intentions, we become masters of our lives and find ourselves less likely to spend time in pain and suffering.

Energy is vibrating around us at all times, pulling us toward the realization of our highest and best.

Although it appears that we pray for a response from God, the Truth is that prayer is in response to God's urgings toward us. Because we are Spiritual Beings growing through a human experience, prayer is a movement of spirit toward Spirit—energy toward Energy.

Every one of us affects the reality that we see; therefore, it seems pertinent to our exploration that we take a look at what we mean by *reality.*

What is Reality?

The experience of ourselves beyond the physical and in perfect union with the Divine; the realm of absolute Truth; the stream which sets out from the heart of God returns home again.[76]

There are two aspects of reality: (1) that which we experience around us based on our five senses and (2) that which exists at the level of Absolute Truth and is changeless and based on immutable laws. When speaking about them, we use a capital "R" for the second one to differentiate it from the first.

What we experience with our five senses is primarily based on many internal and external factors; such as emotions, past experiences, beliefs, and indoctrination. We rarely, if ever, experience what is happening presently without some influence by one or more of these and, because of that, our experiences are usually changing and difficult to predict.

When we are experiencing Reality, from the perspective of the principles of Truth, we are not at the whims of the senses, but live in the knowledge that Truth, Order and Perfection are playing out in the invisible realm; thus, causing a shift in consciousness that facilitates a shift in our paradigm.

What is a Paradigm?

The dictionary defines paradigm as "a model, example or pattern" of something. The word *paradigm* comes from the Greek word *paradeigma,* which is formed by two words:

---

[76] Evelyn Underhill, <u>Mysticism</u>, 1911

para, meaning "along side of or beyond" and *deigma,* meaning "example." Another term for the word *paradigm* is "worldview."

A *Paradigm,* then, is an overarching perspective held by a majority that drives the current culture; the prevailing collective consciousness or belief system. It can also be a familial, cultural, theological or professional pattern or perspective. In other words, it is a belief system espoused by a group of people that determines or impacts the choices they make and the way they live their lives. Our paradigms are formed by what we perceive as our reality based on the views, beliefs and traditions with which we have aligned.

In prayer, our paradigm may be based on what we believe God (Creator) is, who we believe we are, what our relationship to God is and how God responds or does not respond to our prayers. As we grow spiritually, a paradigm shift may be required (and may even occur naturally) in order to encompass our expanded viewpoint. For example, we have grown up believing that God was a being in the sky that blessed or punished and answered our prayers in accordance with our behavior. As our theological perspective changes, it causes a paradigm shift that brings us to the Reality that God is energy, principle, unchanging law and exists within each of us as us.

When we pray from the little "r" reality, we are never really certain whether or not our prayers will be answered; however, when we pray from the capital "R" Reality, we are assured that all prayer is answered, which brings us back to the first premise of what you may not know about prayer.

We create our reality—we *are* reality—we are producing machines. If you don't believe it, look around at our world—your world—and see what we have created.

In his book, *Dancing Wu-Li Masters,* Gary Zukav offers this superb perspective on **Reality**:

REALITY

"Reality" is what we take to be true.
What we take to be true is what we believe.
What we believe is based upon our perceptions.
What we perceive depends upon what we look for.
What we look for depends upon **what we think.**

What we think depends upon what we perceive.
What we perceive determines what we believe.
What we believe determines what we take to be true.
What we take to be true is our **"Reality!"**

So when we talk about **Quantum Prayer,** we are referring to the utilization of our relationship with the quantum field of energy (of which we are part and particle) to create the Reality we desire to experience rather than the reality created randomly by unconscious participation in the activity of creation.

How do we consciously participate in the activity of co-creating with the Quantum Field?

First, it requires some knowledge about what the Quantum Field is and how it operates; then it requires a paradigm shift in order to align with Reality.

The *Quantum Field* is the invisible realm of energy particles that, when their vibratory rate slows down, appear as matter in the visible realm. It is the field of infinite possibilities. It is the quarry from which substance is mined. When we engage with it, those particles become waves and begin moving toward the shore of manifestation.

The *Quantum Field* works according to universal scientific principles and immutable laws that govern its behavior. Because we are one with it, we are endowed with the power to manipulate it and govern it to attain mastery over our lives.

A *Paradigm Shift* is required in order to move beyond our limited perceptions and beliefs about who we are and what Reality/reality is in order to align ourselves with its awesome power. Because what we focus on is what we draw to us, we must learn to shift our perception beyond what is apparent to the five senses to foster a belief in what we cannot see, yet know is the Truth—Absolute Reality.

What is Absolute Reality?

Absolute Reality is the Truth that God (Source, I Am) expresses through us as perfection, wholeness, health, prosperity, peace and love; that when anything other than that is manifested, it is because our focus is still in the reality of the five senses and not on the Truth.

There is no gray area in the *Absolute*. Truth cannot be wishy-washy; it is the same now as it always was and forever will be.

Most commonly, when we manifest what we do not want, there is an interference from the Core Negative Beliefs residing in the subconscious mind. These Core Negative Beliefs (I am unworthy; I'm not good enough; I never succeed; no one is there for me; I'm alone; life is hard; etc.) cancel out our strongest intentions and most fervent affirmative prayers. We must heal these if we are to diminish their power in our lives.

How do we heal our Core Negative Beliefs?

How do we heal them? By forgiving those who taught them to us and believing, instead, that we are beloved sons and daughters of God, in whom God is well-pleased, and who deserve living in the Kingdom of Heaven right here and right now.

So what's the point of it all anyway?

We are, as Dr. Fred Alan Wolfe says, "dancing on the edge of chaos" and we are also on the threshold of a global awakening that will close the gap between science and religion. There are many hints throughout the teachings of scripture from the Bible, the Koran, the Bhagavad Gita, the Torah and many other ancient scriptures that reveal this is so.

Jesus said *The Kingdom of Heaven is at hand* (Matt 3:2; Matt 4:17; Matt 10:7) and *The Kingdom of God is within you*.

Quantum Physics says we are the creators of our world. Yet, we look around us and see hunger, homelessness, poverty, war, and pain and suffering everywhere. If it is true that we create our world, that we are co-creators with Source and that we are the force that activates energy from particles of possibility to manifest matter, we are being called to create the world we wish to see; in other words, to take matters into our own hands.

Our purpose is to turn Hell into Heaven[77].

DIVINE LIGHT, COME FORTH
POUR YOURSELF INTO ME
OPEN MY MIND TO THE LOVE THAT I AM
FILL ME WITH THE AWARENESS OF MY
PERFECT SELF
I AM YOUR WILLING VESSEL

---

[77] *A Course in Miracles* (CA: Fdn. For Inner Peace 1975, 1985, 1992)

PAUSE FOR REFLECTION & STUDY

At this time I invite you to take some time to reflect on what you have read so far, if you wish, and allow these concepts to settle within your heart and your mind. If you are part of a Book Study Group, this may be a good time for discussion. Below are some Study Questions to assist you:

 Why is it necessary to forgive before going into prayer and meditation?

 What would be the necessity in having an understanding of Quantum Physics in order to deepen your prayer practice?

 What is the difference between "reality" and "Reality"? How does that affect your prayer practice?

 How does changing our paradigm affect how we co-create during prayer?

 What do our Core Negative Beliefs have to do with our reality?

 How can we be absolutely sure that our prayers are being answered?

Brethren, pray for us.

How Do We Pray for Other People?

In praying with and for others, we recognize the Divinity within them and within all life, no matter what the appearances are. We must know and affirm that each person is created in the image and likeness of God.

In praying with and for others, we must not get trapped by the negative things we see and hear. It is essential that we see beyond the situation or condition to the Truth of their Being. They are made in the image and likeness of God; they are perfect in spite of their flaws; and they, too, embody the Christ within them.

> *"The greatest gift we can ever give to anyone, the most helpful thing we can ever do for another is to trust the power of God in that person, to have faith that with this power all things are possible, all disease is curable, all conditions are capable of transformation."*[78]

Before we pray with or for someone, it is critical that we first pray for ourselves. We do this to clear away any doubt within ourselves; to receive illumination, peace, understanding and deeper Faith in the power of God. We need to have total Trust in the power of prayer and the all-good, all-knowing, everywhere-present power of God.

When we pray for another, it has an equal affect on us.

---

[78] (Martha Smock, *Meet it With Faith*, (Missouri: Unity Books, 1966, 1982), p. 110.

James Dillet Freeman says, *"I cannot pray for myself without praying for my brother, and I cannot pray for my brother without praying for my enemy. For prayer is that which unites me with God, and the nearer I draw to God, the nearer I draw to my fellows."*[79]

We may have a tendency to pray for others without first praying for ourselves, without realizing how important it is to first center ourselves in spirit. Only in this way can we become open and receptive to allow God's power to flow through us.

And I, when I am lifted up from the earth, will draw all men unto me. (John 12:32 RSV)

Finally, in praying with and for others we must truly let go and let God. God knows what is best for the person for whom we are praying.

We cannot have any investment in the outcome. Once we have prayed, know that it is now in God's hands and let it go. Many times we say we're giving things over to God, and then we keep peeking to see if it is done yet.

"A watched pot never boils." If you have to keep checking—keep asking—you don't completely trust God. You still believe you have to do something. People who are *controlling* have a difficult time with letting go and letting God.

"Whenever you pray for others, have faith that there is a Spirit in them, a Spirit that is God, a Spirit that will not fail. The way in which God guides others may be different from the way in which you think they should go. But if you are

---

[79] James Dillet Freeman, *Prayer: The Master Key*, (Missouri: Unity Books, 1976) p. 132.

praying in faith, if you are trusting the power of God, then you are able to let go of what you personally think should be the outcome, the answer. You are willing to let God's will be done, for you know that God's will is good, perfect, and true. "[80]

When you are praying for another who is in the midst of a storm, focus first on that calm center at the eye of the storm and see it as the center of their being. Hold in your heart and consciousness that they are aligned with that place of poise, and know that God walks with them and calms the troubled waters.

---

[80] Martha Smock, *Meet it With Faith*, (Missouri: Unity Books, 1966, 1982), p. 88.

Pray without ceasing.

(1Th 5:17 KJVA)

Some Useful Tools for Strengthening Our Prayer Life

Although, ultimately, we each develop a prayer method and practice that is right and perfect for us individually, when we are just beginning, some basic tools that incorporate structure can provide us with a foundation.

Just as the outgrowth of a seed depends upon the soil in which it is planted, the outcome of our prayers is supported by the soil of the consciousness that creates it. If the soil is *fear* or *doubt,* the prayer sent forth will only align with that energy and not the Divine Order and Infinite Possibilities of the *Grand Operational Design*

With this in mind, I have included a couple of practices recommended by *Unity Worldwide Ministries* and the *Unity Institute* to provide you with structured process with which to begin designing your Life of Prayer. These processes are not meant to be considered as *required* but, rather, as *useful.* You will know when your own prayer practice supercedes them.

Myrtle Fillmore, in the book *Myrtle Fillmore's Healing Letters*, outlines a 7-day Formula for 'treating" a condition or holding a spiritual thought that I have found extremely helpful.

1. Monday—Statement of Being; repeat the ideal frequently.

2. Tuesday—Denials; deny the power of the condition over you throughout the day.

3. Wednesday—Affirmation; affirm the Absolute Truth of Being.

4. Thursday—Faith; declare your faith in the perfect outcome and your "right" to receive what is yours by Divine Birthright.

5. Friday—Speak the Word; declare every word an effective, working agent for good.

6. Saturday—Praise; declare your perfection in the eyes of a loving and compassionate Source and give praise to your Source.

7. Sunday—Silence; wait in the Silence upon the words of Spirit.

Myrtle says this formula may also be used to "treat" others.

Additionally, Unity teaches a 5-Step Prayer Method to assist the beginning prayer student in creating a daily practice.

The *5-Step Method* is very similar to that of a Religious Science *Treatment* and is the process that helped me create my own Life of Prayer.

5-Step Prayer Method

1. **RELAXATION:**
   Find a quiet, comfortable place for prayer and meditation. Relax your mind and your body. Take several deep, cleansing breaths. Allow sufficient time to relax and release tension. Detach yourself from the outer-world conditions, cares and concerns.

2. **CONCENTRATION:**

   Center your attention upon the indwelling presence of God. Create an altar in consciousness where you are totally devoted to God and bow to His Will. Call forth the Holy Spirit

3. **MEDITATION:**
   Begin the focus upon a spiritual idea, sacred thought or an inspirational passage. Align yourself with the presence and power of Spirit. Open yourself to experience the presence of God and to *hear* the "still small voice."

4. **REALIZATION:**
   Go into the silence and still the inner activity. In the silence, our mind is open and receptive to Divine Ideas. Become aware of the "still small voice." *Know* the presence of God in, through, around and as you. *Listen*

5. **THANKSGIVING:**
   Give thanks in advance for your good—your demonstration, recognizing God as the source of all your good, and *knowing* that your prayer is answered even before you ask.

PAUSE FOR REFLECTION & STUDY

At this time I invite you to take some time to reflect on what you have read so far, if you wish, and allow these concepts to settle within your heart and your mind. If you are part of a Book Study Group, this may be a good time for discussion. Below are some Study Questions to assist you:

- Is there any thread of unforgiveness left within you that might detract from the power of your prayers?

- What is your understanding of forgiveness?

- Have you forgiven yourself?

- When praying, how do we stay focused on a positive outcome and not the current condition?

- What does it mean to pray without ceasing?

- Did you find any new tools that will help strengthen your prayer life? If so, which?

And God is able to make all grace abound toward you, that in everything,
always having all self-sufficiency, you may abound to every good work;
(2 Corinthians 9:8 MKJV)

Grace

"The more we pray, the more we experience the grace of God, until
we finally realize that we live by grace."[81]

After all is said and done, what really supports us in the midst of our own recklessness, foolishness and stubbornness, is God's unfailing *Grace*.

Grace is like a get-out-of-jail-free card. It is that loving essence of God that looks beyond our attempts to hit the mark and the many times we "miss the mark," and looks instead at our divine birthright as sons and daughters of God. We are so precious and important to God that we are forgiven for our behavior and offered preemptive redemption.

Grace is what gives us a chance in spite of ourselves.

Various dictionaries define *Grace* as "a favor." In other words, God is doing us a favor. We may not be strictly adhering to the laws of God, but God is doing us "a favor" by diminishing the effect of the original cause.

I look at *Grace* as *Lagniappe* (pronounced *lan-yap*). In Louisiana, where I was raised, when someone gives you a little more than what you paid for we call it *Lagniappe*. God's *Grace* is just a little something extra. We didn't really do anything to earn it; we just got it as "a favor."

---

[81] Hypatia Hasbrouck, *Handbook of Positive Prayer*, (Missouri: Unity Books, 1984, 1989, 1995), p. 143.

In my prayer classes, I tell my students that *Grace* is what prevents us from experiencing the full impact of the remuneration from Universal Laws before we know better.

It is sort of like driving a car in Manhattan as a visitor to New York from California and you don't know the traffic laws there. You get to a red light; you stop and, then after checking carefully, you make a right turn. A policeman pulls you over and tells you that you just made an illegal turn; however, you show him your driver's license and tell him that in California a right turn on a red light is legal. Instead of giving you a $200 traffic ticket, he gives you a $25 citation or maybe even a written warning. If, however, the same thing occurs and you have a New York driver's license, and you say you didn't know that making a right turn on a red light was illegal, he will laugh all the way to his car or motorcycle where he writes out that $200 ticket.

In the first scenario you didn't know so the repercussion is a little thump upside the head. In the second scenario you did know, and did it anyway, so you experienced a cosmic two-by-four.

> Hypatia Hasbrouck says, *"Grace is God's gift of love and mercy, given freely to us whether or not we deserve it. We cannot steal, borrow, buy, or earn it. We can only accept or refuse it."*[82]

How do we accept or refuse *Grace?*

We accept it by the realization that we are Blessed; that we have been pulled out of the mouth of the Lion many times;

---

[82] Ibid.

that we have, fortunately, not reaped what we have sown in many instances; and that many of God's wondrous gifts have been bestowed upon us in spite of our unwillingness to listen and obey.

We refuse it by our inability to realize that something greater than we are—something loving and generous—is sustaining us and providing for us even when we cannot see it and even when we make mistakes.

I believe *Grace* comes from the very heart of God that knows only love and when we allow our own hearts to be open to receiving, giving and being love, it is the gentle goodnight kiss of a loving parent while we slumber.

God's *Grace* is always present and available to us. It is that all-sustaining energy in which we "live and move and have our being."[83]

Grace is a blessing that is poured out upon us in astonishing ways and bestowed upon us abundantly. When we recognize and accept it, we are prepared to meet any circumstance with ease because we know that we move through life always prepared.

We can also make a conscious effort to have that *Grace* flow freely into our lives by aligning ourselves with the wisdom and guidance of God. We can desire to "know God more" and have that show up and bless us. We can realize and know that God cares about us, regardless of our current circumstances. When we hold that consciousness, we create an arena in which *Grace* has an open invitation to work its miraculous ways.

---

[83] Acts 17:28 MKJV.

A consistent prayer life is a powerful way to create an arena for *Grace*. As we grow in divine consciousness through prayer, we are renewed and restored into our rightful place in the Kingdom of God.

Charles Fillmore, Unity's co-founder says that *Grace* is our "aid from God in the process of regeneration."[84]

We can rest assured, beloved ones, that our mistakes along the path of "regeneration" are never held against us. Grace is our covenant with God that we will always be taken care of.

> The Gospels tell us: *For the Law came through Moses, but grace and truth came through Jesus Christ.* [85]

Jesus opened the door for Grace and its transforming power through the work he did while here on earth, by continually telling us and showing us that we all are sons and daughters of God, that God loves all of us and that we have the ability to continue the works he started here and *"even greater."*[86]

By believing in the works that Jesus did, believing the things he told us, and applying these things to every aspect of our lives, we enter into that same consciousness with Jesus and the Christ is awakened within us and restored to every part of the Kingdom where we live under that Blessed Assurance that Grace bestows.

---

[84] Charles R. Fillmore, *The Revealing Word* (Missouri: Unity Books 1959), p. 88.
[85] John 1:17 MKJV.
[86] John 14:12 MKJV.

Exercise:

Affirm daily "The Grace of God is my assurance
that I am loved."

Know that *Grace* is ever affirming our oneness with
God and with each other, and that we are always under
its protection. Accept it with full knowing and prepare to
receive it abundantly.

Grace is that shelter you happen upon when you get caught
in a storm.

And lead us not into temptation, but deliver us from evil: For thine is the kingdom, and the power, and the glory, for ever. Amen.

(Mat 6:13 KJVA)

Amen

Most prayers end with *Amen*. *Amen* is the period at the end of the sentence, the crossing of the "Ts" and the dotting of the "I's." *Amen* is the affirmation that God's Will is done before it appears before us.

Amen comes from a Hebrew word meaning "verily, so it is, so shall it be and so be it." It is a seal upon the agreement we have made with God to wait, listen and have faith in the outworking of Divine Order.

Webster's Dictionary defines *Amen* as "used to express solemn ratification (as of an expression of faith) or hearty approval (as of an assertion).[87]

By saying *Amen* at the end of our prayers, we are confirming that God is the Source and we are the channels. We are acknowledging that our good comes from God and that we trust in the all-providing Goodness of God. In effect, we are completely certain of the outcome.

Amen may also be used as a subliminal message to our consciousness to surrender to God all that we have requested to be carried out in God-Indwelling's own wise and wonderful way.

In the midst of the storm, *Amen* is the trust that carries us through until the sun shines again.

Amen.

---

[87] Webster's Ninth New Collegiate Dictionary, 1988 by Merriam-Webster.

Now the God of peace be with you all. Amen.

(Rom 15:33 KJVA)

One Final Word

As you begin to read and use the prayers in this book, there are two fundamental things to remember about prayer: (1) There is always an answer to prayer—when you understand how prayer works and have learned how to use it; and (2) To receive that answer, you must prepare your heart and mind to support you in reaching that state of consciousness where the meeting point with God exists.

Basically, however, just remember that you are an idea in the mind of God and with that status comes the assurance that your every need is being met. All you have to do is be willing.

"Faith and willingness to receive are the conditions under which our prayers are brought into visible answer."[88]

May your prayers be lifted up on the wings of Angels and soar into the endless substance of God, returning to you loaded with bountiful blessings and absolute joy.

Prayer is something deeper than words. It is present in the soul before it has been formulated in words. And it abides in the soul after the last words of prayer have passed over our lips. (O. Hallesby)

---

[88] Myrtle Fillmore, *How to Let God Help You*, (Missouri: Unity Books, 1956), p. 170.

PAUSE FOR REFLECTION & STUDY

At this time I invite you to take some time to reflect on what you have read so far, if you wish, and allow these concepts to settle within your heart and your mind. If you are part of a Book Study Group, this may be a good time for discussion. Below are some Study Questions to assist you:

- When have you seen the activity of *Grace* in your own life?

- Is all prayer answered? How?

- If we do not see our prayers manifest, what has happened or not happened?

- What keeps us from healing ourselves? What change could we make that would expand the possibility and assure the desired outcome?

- Why do we stay locked in an appearance of lack? How do we break free?

- What is the most important thing to remember when praying for others?

Spiritual Nutrition:
Prayers for Our Daily Life

This section of the book contains prayers that readers of the EmpowerMag column, Message for the Miracle Minded, have enjoyed over the last few years. I offer them to you as temporary tools to support you in your prayer life, until your own prayers begin to flow forth from Divine Mind.

Based on the studies of the Silent Unity prayer ministry, showing that the millions of prayers they receive fall into five major categories (healing, prosperity, guidance, forgiveness and general), I have categorized these prayers to assist you in quickly locating the prayer you need at any given moment.

I have added one more category "For Our Loved Ones," because praying for others is one of the most powerful activities of prayer we can express. Many of the prayers in this section were written for my personal family and friends in their time of challenge.

In this new edition, I have added prayers I have shared on my web page and others that were written in response to prayer requests. All names have been removed to maintain confidentiality.

Finally, some of these prayers are recorded on *Light Visions*, my recently released CD of Meditations and Prayers.

Healing Prayers

Is any among you afflicted? Let him pray. Is any cheerful? Let him sing psalms. Is any sick among you? Let him call for the elders of the church, and let them pray over him, anointing him with oil in the name of the Lord.[89]

When we pray for a healing for ourselves or someone else, on a metaphysical level, we are actually praying for the realization that disease is not a natural phenomenon of the Truth of our being; rather, that we have failed to see the perfection that is only possible as sons and daughters of God.

We are praying to change our minds about an erroneous perception. Therefore, when praying for a healing prayer, it is important for us to see beyond the actual condition. If we are unable to hold in our minds the Truth of the situation we are praying for, it is best to ask someone else to pray or wait until we are not so personally attached to the person or situation. Holding the condition in mind while we pray only exacerbates the current results.

Pray knowing that God is wholeness and created only like Itself; therefore, in Absolute Truth, everything is a reflection of that wholeness.

---

[89] James 5:13-14 MKJV

Dear God,

In whom we live, move and have our being, we celebrate our oneness with You and each other. We align every part of us with Your healing energy from the center of our being and see it radiating throughout our bodies, purifying, cleansing and making whole every bone, tissue, cell, nerve, muscle, body part and drop of blood.

As we return to our Source, we return to our wholeness. We extend that wholeness to embrace our homes, families, workplaces, schools, churches, neighborhoods, communities, governments, cities, states and countries that all may be lifted up into the full manifestation of perfect life, perfect peace, perfect health and perfect love.

Regardless of what we see with the human eye, with the "single eye" we hold the vision that was in Christ Jesus and see the Truth: That we are made in Your image and we are perfect.

Forgive us for ever believing that we could be sick and we forgive ourselves for the erroneous thoughts, beliefs and feelings that have caused the out-picturing of anything less than the absolute perfection that You created.

We surrender our will and our way to Your Will and Your Way and we let go of everything that causes us to feel fearful, angry, anxious and untrusting.

We turn over our fear to You and we are aware of Your protecting and loving arms.

We turn over our anger to You and a sweet gentle peace comes over us that passes our human understanding.

We turn over our anxiety to You and realize that You are leading, guiding and directing our every step to a place in consciousness where all is well.

We turn over any mistrust to You and recognize the divinity within all our brothers and sisters, that we may know no harm from them or toward them.

We stand firm in our faith that You are the Source of our Good and we open our hearts and minds to receive that good right here and right now.

Thanking You in advance for what You desire for us and what we know is ours by divine birthright, we are truly grateful. And so it is.

Amen.

Dear God,

I look to You for the perfection of mind, body and spirit. I see beyond the physical appearance of sickness or dis-ease to the Truth of my being—a whole and perfect spiritual being, made in the image and likeness of You.

Send forth Your healing love to move through my body and my affairs, that anything unlike Your perfect love is cast out and no longer has any power over me.

With the guiding hand of the Holy Spirit, I can touch the hem of the radiant garment of the Christ that is the true nature of my being and receive a complete healing right here, right now.

I know that You have heard me and that my prayer is answered, because my faith is planted in Truth and through it the mountains of mortal error are moved into the sea of nothingness from which they came.

I claim perfection. I claim wholeness. I claim love, in the name and after the loving nature of my Brother, Way-Shower and Master Teacher, Jesus the Christ.

And so it is and so it shall be.

Amen

Dear God,

I admit that of myself I am powerless over this condition; but with Your healing love, and through the works demonstrated by Jesus to strengthen me, I can do all things.

I open myself up to the healing energy that is always available to me and I accept the complete manifestation of harmony and wholeness in my mind, body and affairs.

Help me to demonstrate as Jesus did, that I have the faith to see myself whole. If anything exists within my mind, my soul or my life that remains a barrier to a complete healing, I ask Dear God that it be removed right now. I surrender all that I am to You.

May Your Will be done this day in me as it is in Heaven. I am truly grateful. So it is.

Amen.

Sheila Gautreaux

Dear Lord,

Into Your hands we commend our need for healing. Through Your loving eyes, we see the perfect manifestation of wholeness. This condition has no power to override the Truth of our being—that we are free from any appearance of sickness or dis-ease.

Because we are Your children, we have inherited perfect minds, perfect bodies and perfect spirits. To see anything less than that is to forget who we are.

Continue to be with us as we find the strength to move through this process with grace and dignity. Hold us close when our courage falters. Let us feel Your love when it appears that we are alone. Remind us that You will never leave us alone.

In You we trust and through You we rise up in the fulfillment of the Promise of the Kingdom of Heaven right here and right now. We are whole and complete. We know this to be true in the name and after the loving nature of Jesus the Christ.

Amen

Father,

You are always faithful in Your love for me. It is always there, surrounding me and filling me with absolute joy. Even when I cannot love myself, Your love is present and holding the torchlight until I can see the love within. I look to that love now, needing its comfort and care. My own heart has failed me and Your love is all that I need to see me through this bitter moment. I know that if I can catch but a glimmer of that light, the way out of this darkness will be made clear. Remember me, Dear Father, Your child so lost and weary. I lift my eyes to behold you. I raise my hand to Yours, so that I may be lifted up into the Kingdom of Heaven right here, right now.

Amen

Dear God,

There is a great sadness here today, and our resolve is threatening to break. We need courage and strength to make it through the mountains of grief and sorrow. We are feeling the loss of someone dear and cannot see our lives without their presence. Help us to remember that death is not the end, but a new beginning. Show us the way to hold our loved one within our hearts, while releasing them to their new place in your kingdom. Send us the Holy Spirit to comfort us while we find the way back to our joy. Mend our broken hearts that we may love in a brand new way. We are deeply in need of Your peace to rest our weary souls. We open our hearts to you, Dear God, knowing that we will feel whole again.

Amen

Dear God,

We are open and receptive to being the light of love and healing for the United States and our planet. We are willing to heal and be healed at depth.

We forgive ourselves for what we have said or done against brothers and sisters everywhere and against Mother Earth. We offer our deepest apologies and we humbly atone all acts, conscious or unconscious against them.

We commit ourselves from this day forward to living in conscious union with the world. We make an effort to be better men and women in our thoughts, words, actions and choices.

We extend love to every corner of the earth, calling out the shadows that they may be healed. We look upon the innocence of our brothers and sisters and through their eyes we look upon our own innocence.

Together we are healed. Together we walk hand in hand toward a New World Order where love is the answer in every situation, condition and circumstance.

Thanking You in advance for helping us walk this new path, we are truly grateful.

Amen

Infinite Spirit,

I honor my oneness with you. I am ever aware of my connection to Your all-providing, all-empowering, loving presence in my body and in my life experience. I acknowledge Your power in my mind, body, and affairs and in all existence. I acknowledge the perfection in my body. I acknowledge the perfection in my life. I acknowledge the perfection in all creation. I realize my heart's desire through my own divinity. I am so grateful for all the good that always was, that is here right now and is ever unfolding throughout eternity. Thank you God, thank you God, thank you God. And so it is.

Amen

Dear God,

Open our hearts to reveal to us the answers we have hidden away from ourselves. Give us the courage to hear the Truth and the strength to do the work to heal our lives. Thank you very much.

Amen

Father-Mother God,

We acknowledge Your presence and power in us and in everything that exists. We rest assured in our connection to Your presence and open ourselves to feel this at the very depths of our being.

Reveal to us the truths that evade us in the midst of our mindless functioning. Show us Yourself in the eyes of our brothers and sisters. Remind us that the Self looking back at us is the only self we have ever known. Join our hearts with one another that we may feel the unbroken link in the chain of all creation. Pull from us the love we neglect to share and encircle the planet with its healing power. Teach us to be better people that, through our own salvation, the world is uplifted and everything is healed. Support us in standing in Truth in the face of the illusions of adversity. Keep us from the pitfalls created by our haphazard footsteps. Lead us to the Promised Land, where we may dwell with You for all eternity.

Thank you so much. And so it is, and so it shall be.

Amen.

Today, Oh Lord, I pray for others. I pray for the healing, prosperity, guidance, forgiveness and support all of my friends, family, associates and brothers and sisters everywhere are seeking as they strive to know You more along this journey of their lives. May they realize Your love that is always filling their hearts and Your guidance that is always available to them as Your beloved sons and daughters. I pray for the awakening and empowerment of all humanity for the healing of the world. Thank you so much for so much.

Amen.

Our God, Our Light, Our Joy, open our way this week for healing to take place in every aspect of our being and our lives. Heal our bodies that we may continue to work in service to you and all humanity. Heal our minds that we might participate in raising the vibration of the collective consciousness. Heal our spirit so our lives are a living testament to the power of the living Christ. Heal our Nation that it may offer an example of a cooperative spirit in times of challenge. Heal our world that we may avoid repeating the actions that brought us into unnecessary conflict in the past. Most of all, heal our fractured relationships with You so we can heal ourselves.

Amen.

Dear Lord,

Bless me. Bless this Day. Bless everything I do and Bless everyone I encounter. Bless this World and everyone in it. Bless my thoughts and my emotions. Bless the presidential campaign and bless the mother getting her children ready for school. Bless the people involved in the wars around the world and bless the school teacher preparing to welcome her class and shape their young minds. Bless our friends and families and bless our enemies. Bless it all. We know and trust that no matter what, You are good . . . all the time.

Amen

Oh God, our Help in Times of Distress,

We are truly needing Your comfort, Your strength and Your healing love. Forgive us for our fear, but allow us to rest a moment in our grief so we might feel our feelings fully. When You feel the shift in our hearts, help us to move beyond this and step into a greater power and truth than we have ever known before. We know that in You there is no loss. We surrender and trust the process.

Amen.

Father-Mother God, in whom I live and move and have my being, I pray for those who are without jobs and struggling to survive. Give them strength of mind, body and spirit and renew their courage to continue in the face of seemingly impossible odds. Remind them that within them is the power and possibility of their divine birthright as daughters and sons of God, and with this power comes the innate ability to create the possible from the impossible, the unlimited from the limited and the dawning of a new day from the dark night of the soul. Surround them with love, peace and hope and send the Holy Spirit before them to prepare their way for success. Open their hearts to the love I know they have flowing from You in this very moment, allow them to tap into it when things seem to go badly and guide them to lean upon it at every moment. All things are possible to them that love the Lord.

Amen

God, in whom I live and move and have my being, bless me today. Bless my mind, my body and my spirit; bless my thoughts; bless all of my activities; and, more importantly, bless all of my brothers and sisters. Bless the traffic today and especially those who give me the one-fingered wave. Bless my co-workers and the words they speak to and about me and each other. Bless my employers and their success so that they and everyone they employ may continue to thrive. Bless my family and friends, wherever they may be, wherever they may go and hold them close as they move through this day. Bless our country, our world and its leaders, that they may be ever mindful of the great responsibility they have accepted in making decisions that affect the good of the many and not the good of the few. Bless all of your creations large and small. I go forward to greet this day knowing that there is nothing for me to do because you've got it covered and I certainly am grateful about that. Thank you very much.

Amen

Prosperity Prayers

If they obey God and serve him, they live out their lives in peace and prosperity. [90]

When we pray for prosperity for ourselves or someone else, we are seeking to see abundance everywhere. We are taking an active stand against a consciousness of lack and limitation.

Prosperity is having a consciousness of abundance. It is based on the conscious possession of the idea of God's abundance behind of all things. Things come and go, but the idea of abundance endures. Things appear at its command.

Jesus had no visible possessions, but He could supply thousands of persons with food through praising and giving thanks to the invisible Spirit of plenty.

"All things that the Father hath are mine." [91]

True prosperity means many things besides material worth; there is an important difference between spiritual prosperity and material prosperity.

Prosperity manifests itself as we condition our minds through prayer to accept our good.

Frances Foulks in *Effectual Prayer* says "we receive according to our capacity, and the degree of our faith determines our capacity."[92]

The reason we do not manifest prosperity in our lives is because we still hold the erroneous belief system that there

---

[90] Job 36:11 GNB
[91] John 16:15
[92] Frances Foulks, *Effectual Prayer*, (Missouri: Unity Books, 1979, 1986) p. 98

is not enough to go around—we have a consciousness of *lack*.

> *Charles Fillmore said, "Apparently we live in two worlds: an invisible world of thoughts, and a visible world of things. The invisible world of thought substance is the real world, because it is the source of the world of things, and man stands between the two, handing out with his thoughts the unlimited substance of Spirit."*[93]

Another significant block to prosperity is that we fail to understand that giving and receiving are one and the same.

For some of us it is easier to give—we feel guilty receiving. If we cannot receive, it is because we do not freely accept our good or we do not feel worthy to receive.

For one whole day try this exercise: Thank God for everything that you find in your experience; i.e., for the sunrise, birds singing, alarm clock, telephone, car, clouds, friends, your job, etc. You will begin to see what abundance you already have in your world and, by your gratitude, your life will become even more abundant.

God wants us to be prosperous. We used to believe it was a sin to be rich. Actually, it is a sin to be poor.

---

[93] Charles F. Fillmore, *Keep a True Lent*, (Missouri: Unity Books, 1953, 1989) p. 102.

Dear God,

I cannot find my way out of this difficult financial mess alone. I know that I need Your generous love to light my way. I release all worry and concern about my finances and give them over to Your care and keeping. I trust in Your ever-present abundance, knowing that You have already given me all that I need to do all that I need to do. I accept my Divine Inheritance and go forward in faith that I am a prosperous child of a Rich Father. I relinquish all belief in any appearances to the contrary. I thank You in advance for Your loving kindness. So it is.

Amen.

God,

You who are the giver of all that is, move into my heart and open it to the awareness of the abundance that is everywhere present. Teach me how to know that I am being provided for in every time of need. Show me what awaits me when I awaken to Your all-providing goodness and love. I trust You as the Source of all my good, Dear God. Strengthen me when I begin to doubt that this is true. I am Your willing child. Show me the way.

Amen

Sheila Gautreaux

Dear Father-Mother-Everything God,

I surrender all that I am to You. I let go of the need to have, to be, to do and I step into the Allness of Your presence. I release all of my affairs of mind, body and spirit to Your care and keeping. I allow the power that emanates from You to fill my life and express itself in all that manifests in the outer. I breathe in the calming, mindful flow of peace and my world is peaceful. I absorb the transforming, healing flow of love and my world is love-filled. I embrace the ever-present enriching flow of abundance and my world is prosperous. I take in all that You are and my world reflects all that I AM.

Amen

Dear God,

I open my heart to receive Your Love;
I open my mind to receive Your Truth;
I open my spirit to receive Your Power;
And I open my consciousness to receive the endless prosperity that manifests through Your Love, Truth and Power.

I thank You in advance for all the good that always was, that is here right now, and is ever unfolding in my life now.

Amen

Dear God,

Now is the time to release those things we have feared being without, thought we couldn't do without or felt diminished without having them. Help us to see that the only thing we cannot do without is YOU. Be here now in our time of doubt and hesitation. Pry our fingers away from what no longer serves us so that we are able to reach for the blessing You have promised. We are willing.

Amen.

Dear God,

Today I am grateful for my finances regardless of what they currently reflect. I am grateful for bills, creditors and account balances in whatever condition they presently exist. I am grateful because I know that You are the source of my supply and You never run out of anything, and You are always providing me with all that I require. I trust in You and the abundance that is of You. I turn my mind and my eye away from all outer evidence of lack and limitation and turn within to the unlimited supply of good that is my Divine Birthright. Thank you, Dear God, in advance for the perfection that is my finances. I am so grateful.

Amen

Dear Lord,

As I open my eyes and see the beautiful morning You have created I am filled with love and awe at the abundance around me at every moment. Forgive me for those moments that I fall into lack, whining about what I don't have, when there is so much to be grateful for. Today help me see Your abundance in my life and remind me to be grateful in spite of the current situation in my life and in our nation. Help us as a nation to raise our eyes away from the appearance of the condition and look up to our true source, which is You. Support us in standing in love and having compassion for the circumstances of all humanity around the world so that we are in alignment with the Law and attract our good to us in a powerful way. We are prosperous. We are abundantly blessed. You are the source of our supply. There is no lack or limitation. We are prosperous.

Amen

Guidance

"Trust in the Lord with all thine heart, and lean not unto thine own understanding. In all thy ways acknowledge him, and he shall direct thy paths."[94]

When we pray for guidance for ourselves, we are calling forth the wisdom of the universe to provide us with insights through increased intuition. When we pray for others, we are seeking to open them up to be receptive to the wisdom that is always guiding and directing.

The Voice for God is always guiding and directing us; we often don't hear it. The voice of the ego is always guiding and directing us; we often submit to it.

To practice recognizing God's guidance, for thirty days pray only this: "God I want to know you more." Pay attention to what happens in your life and watch the miracles come.

Through prayer and meditation, we surrender to the Will and the Way of Spirit and open ourselves up to be shown the way to our highest, greatest and most perfect good.

---

[94] Proverbs 3:5-6, KJV

Dear God,

In whom we live and move and have our Being, we resolve to know You more.

In this new year, we direct our hearts, minds, bodies and spirits toward a more conscious union with You, by letting our words be Your words, by letting our thoughts be only of You, and by letting our decisions be made in alignment with Your Will.

We love and trust You, Oh Jehovah-Jireh, knowing that the gifts of the Kingdom are Your desire for us. We receive our courage from Your omnipotence. We receive our support from Your omnipresence. We receive our guidance from Your omniscience. We are warmed by Your love and sustained by Your merciful kindness.

Help us to clear away the noise that shatters the crystal clarity of Your "still small voice" that we may hear what You would have us do, where You would have us go, what You would have us say and to whom. God Bless us one and all.

Amen.

Father,

As I begin my busy day, show me where Your Will might best be done. Lead me along peaceful paths and make clear the rough and untrodden places. Be my feet, be my hands, be my ears, be my sight. Help me to see where there is need. Let me hear every call for love. Allow me to touch where healing is needed. Guide me where You want me to be, so that I may do what You want me to do. I am open and receptive to Your guidance and direction. Your Will is mine and my will is Thine. I live to serve you, dear Lord.

Amen.

Dear God,

I have doubted Your goodness, misinterpreted Your guidance, listened to the wrong voices and allowed myself to become hardened of heart to the needs of my brothers and sisters. I have focused too long on the outer trappings and temptations of the physical world and have given too little attention to the Christ that lives in me. I have not always been as kind, loving, fair or truthful as you would have me be. I apologize for these mistakes and accept your unconditional love and forgiveness. Give me always the courage to face the truth about myself, the humility to seek Your forgiveness, the willingness to accept Your grace and the power to be the person I was meant to be. Through the power, life, light, love, authority and victory of Jesus the Christ may I act in all ways as He did. Thank you, Dear God. Amen.

Dearest God,

Lead us into Your ways. Direct us in our understanding that we may be guided by Your "still small voice" and fulfill the purpose for which we were born into this human existence. May we be ever mindful of what is truly Your Will for our lives. Keep us out of the midst of chaos and self-destruction. Remind us that we are one with You now as we have always been. Pull us back from the edges of the deep and painful abyss into which we frequently find ourselves falling. Send us the arm of Jesus to lean upon when it is too difficult to walk of our own accord. Send the Holy Spirit to comfort us when the pain is too intense and the sorrow too profound to bear alone. When the way gets dark and we lose our way, gently guide us back onto the path to our home with You in Heaven.

Amen.

Father-Mother God,

We acknowledge Your presence and Your power in every aspect of our lives. We release the need to be right and allow ourselves to be happy. We resist the temptation to indulge in criticism, condemnation or judgment against our brothers and sisters, and rest in the knowledge that everything created by You is good and perfect. We step away from our mundane thoughts and open our minds to thinking in the realm of love for the uplifting of all humankind. We surrender all that we have, all that we are and all that we have been to the Holy Spirit that the bridge may be rebuilt to once again enjoy the perfect existence with You as it was in the beginning. Now and forever more, we are Your loving children and we are grateful for this gift. And so it is.

Amen.

Dearest God,

I am now faced with a challenge that is beyond my own human comprehension and ability, so I turn to You and surrender myself completely to Your will and Your way.

Remove the fear within my heart and replace it with courage and love. Remove the doubt from my mind and replace it with wisdom and trust. Remove the pain from my soul and replace it with your Blessed Assurance.

If I have hurt anyone in my blindness to the truth of their divinity, forgive me. If I am harboring any ill will toward another, forgive me. If there is any unforgiveness lurking anywhere within my mind, body or soul, free me from the grip of its bondage and let me be free to love, honor and respect all humanity as my brothers and sisters.

I do not ask that this bitter cup be removed, but that I can find its sweetness and savor its nourishing substance. Let there be light, dear God. Help me to see beyond the illusion before me and trust that You are in the process.

Here is my hand, my heart and my life. They are Yours to do with as You will. I trust in You and I trust the process.

Amen

Sheila Gautreaux

Dear God:

Lead, guide and direct me in Your ways, that I may be a living example of Your love for all of Your sons and daughters.

Provide me with the wisdom and insight to make choices that are in alignment with Your Will.

Make me more sensitive to my Brother's needs so I may willingly support his purpose.

Fill me with compassion, as I walk among the suffering of the world; yet, let me not see only the suffering, but let me see as You see—let me see Perfection and Beauty.

When I come upon the darkness, give me the courage to set my light blazing in the sky as a beacon to those seeking the way.

Forgive me for those moments when I forget who I am.

And when my faith begins to waiver, send the Holy Spirit to remind me that You are never farther away than a thought.

Thank you for the love so freely given that we all may dwell within it each and every moment of each and every day.

For this, I am eternally grateful.

Amen

Come Holy Spirit,

Fill me with thy loving presence, so that I may be fortified with love, wisdom, guidance and strength. It is difficult to see the way right now, but I rest assuredly in the knowledge that Your vision always beholds with perfection. My body sometimes fails me, but I am ever certain that your comforting touch is constantly upon me, soothing away the aches and pains. I feel uncertain in moments of challenge, but I can count on Your love to ease the doubts and fears. Many times it appears that my prayers fall on deaf ears, but in my heart I know You always hear me and maintain an open channel between me and the Source of all my good. With gratitude, I accept the love, wisdom, guidance and strength that flow into me in a steady stream in this moment and all the moments to come. For this, I am truly grateful

Amen

Divine Light

Be my guide when the way is dark. Illumine my mind to see the way clear to my highest good. Allow me to know Your Will for me. Keep me centered in my divinity. Forgive me when I am so busy listening to the self-centered urgings of my ego that I do not hear Your voice guiding me to make right choices. Remind me that I am a child of God, when the human of me forgets its birthright. Look favorably upon me as I struggle, when struggle is unnecessary and futile. Take my hand and lead me out of the muck and mire into which I have placed myself through my own foolishness. Show me where the exit is when I have locked myself into old negative habits. Wake me when I have fallen asleep and cannot awaken from the nightmare. Help me in my own helplessness. And, all else failing in my stubbornness, grab me by the collar and snatch me back from the edge of the cliff.

Thank you!

Amen

Dear God,

"Glorify thou me with thine own self with the glory which I had with thee before the world was."

I surrender my will and my way that I may be lifted from the appearances before me to see the Truth that Your goodness and mercy is always moving in, through and around me and everything I experience.

I offer my heartfelt commitment to doing the works that glorify You, so that my life is a living testimony to Your goodness. I have faith that your love for me is true and that you are always acting on my behalf in mind, body and spirit.

Guide me in the direction You want me to go, instruct me in what You want me to do, place in my mouth the words You want me to speak and lead me to those to whom You want me to speak them.

May all that I think, speak and do reflect the magnificence available to all of Your children in Your kingdom and may I be a living example that this possibility lives within each and every one of them.

By Your love, I am nurtured; by Your truth, I am inspired; by Your guidance, I am directed; and by Your grace, I am lifted up from the depths of despair into the full glory of an Heir to the Kingdom.

I humbly accept Your will for me to fulfill the purpose for which I came into the world. I will go wherever You lead me willingly.

Amen.

Divine Spirit,

We open our hearts to receive the pure love that never fails to fulfill. We surrender to the Will that knows us at depth. We trust the process that is always certain. We accept the gifts that always bless. We focus our total desire upon knowing this experience of You in the deepest realms of our being and we submerge ourselves in the pure rapture this Knowing brings. We stand before You naked and stripped bare of all that stands between us and pure realization. We meld into your perfect essence and we rejoice at the loss of all that we were before. Our love for you consumes our very souls and we move beyond time and space into the endless stream of all that is. Through this we are made whole and by this we are no less than all that You are. We are grateful. So be it.

Amen.

To the Force within me, from which all expression is shared, and with which I align my seeking soul.

I am grateful for this very moment in time that opens the gateway to the potential from which my individualized expression has been extended, to capture the greater realization that pursues enlightenment.

I surrender to the way of the Master Teacher, Christ Jesus, who is witness to my seeking and points the way to the evolution of my own Christhood.

All that I am from limitation to revelation is given over to the Holy Spirit to be molded and shaped according to the template of perfection from which I was created. I open my heart to receive the situations, circumstances and teachers who await my single word of "surrender" to lovingly guide me through the path of initiation into full Discipleship. I am willing to have the very last remnants of those things that have kept me in bondage burned away by the purifying power of the Holy Spirit, that I may live a life totally engaged in the way of Truth.

It is my greatest desire to love all of humanity, honor all of creation and offer compassion to even those whom my perception believes are the "least of these." To this beginning I surrender my heart, my thoughts, my beliefs, my actions, my feelings, my desires and my very being. Break away the final resistance and offer me to the Holy Experience that brings the ecstasy that exists beyond the limited ability of my human comprehension.

Let me fall into You, Dear One. I am willing.

Amen

Lord God,

I welcome in this new year, knowing that with You all things are made new and whatever has been ailing, failing or flailing is now renewed, revitalized and reenergized as I allow You to show me the way. That is my New Year's wish, Dear Lord, to turn everything over to You this year and surrender my own feeble efforts to make things happen my way. You have prepared before me a table filled with a bounty of good things—prosperity, perfect health, perfect peace, good relationships, joy and a wonderful life—and all I have to do is "choose" and "accept." Let me not wander off looking at another's table or seeing how I could set up a better table; help me "choose" what is right and perfect for the life You have designed with me. I am willing to be an open channel for Your guidance, direction and insights. Touch me Lord, that I may have a new year like no other that has come before and the best life I have ever had. I "choose" it and I "accept" it. I thank You for it because I know that I have already received it.

Amen.

Forgiveness

But whenever you stand praying, if you have a grievance against any one, forgive it, so that your Father in Heaven may also forgive you your offences."[95]

When we pray for forgiveness for ourselves, or others, we are asking that we might see beyond the act to the innocence of the one committing the act.

While it may be true that someone has committed a heinous act against us, we remember that we are all sons and daughters of our Creator and made in that image and likeness. If our Creator is All-Good and we are the image and likeness of that Good, then at the core of our Being, we are good; therefore, the one committing the act is—in Truth—good.

By praying to forgive the person, we are not condoning the act. We are forgiving them for not remembering who they are and, in that forgetfulness, expressing behavior that is out of integrity with the Truth of their Being.

Often, the most difficult person to forgive is our self. Self-forgiveness is the first step in opening the door to all forgiveness. Even if we can forgive another, if we have not forgiven ourselves the consciousness of "unforgiveness" is still very much inherent within us and is blocking the flow of our good in every aspect of our mind, body and affairs.

Here is an exercise to help activate the power of forgiveness in your life:

1. Make a list of everyone you have, or may have, caused any harm (even if they don't know about it) and of everyone who has, or may have, caused you any harm.

---

[95] Mark 11:25 WNT

2. For each name on the list, say three times: "The forgiving love of the Christ in me cleanses me of all past mistakes; I am whole and free. As I fully and freely forgive myself and others, so, in turn, am I fully and freely forgiven.

3. Continue doing this until you no longer feel any anger, hurt, pain, anxiety or other physical sensations in your body.

Let your forgiveness prayers be heartfelt, expressing a deep desire to release whatever you hold against yourself or another, and then you will have truly forgiven and been forgiven.

A favorite forgiveness prayer is one by the late Unity Minister and teacher, Imelda Shanklin:

O God of love and forgiveness, love and forgive in me.

All that has offended me I forgive. Whatever has made me bitter, unhappy or restless, I forgive. From henceforth, I shall remember that Thy spirit animating me and all others is perfect and holy, that Thy presence makes this planet heaven.

I forgive everything that I have remembered as offense; I forgive everything by which, not remembering, I may have been offended. If there be in the depths of subconsciousness that which holds itself as offense, I forgive; I let it go, and can no more be offended by it.

I forgive, that Thy love may cleanse my soul; that Thy life may flow through my flesh and make me again to be the undisguised image and likeness. I forgive my ignorance of the past, and from this moment I hold Thy mind to be my mind, that the light eternal may make bright the paths of my soul. Within and without, things past, things present, and things to come, I forgive, I forgive, I forgive."

Selected Studies, Imelda Octavia Shanklin

Dear God,

Help me to surrender my belief in judgment, revenge and vindication over a wrong that has been committed against me and toward the brother or sister who has committed this act.

Open my heart to the depths of its love as demonstrated many times by Jesus.

Release me from the grip of hurt, pain and disappointment that I may release my brother/sister from the prison of unforgiveness in which I have incarcerated him/her.

Allow me to remove the log from my eyes that I may behold the radiant innocence of my brother/sister.

Forgive me for my misperceptions and for failing to recognize my own innocence in my brother/sister.

I place any residual feelings that are not in alignment with true love, in Your hands.

I release and let go of my own selfish desires and surrender to the desires You hold within Your loving nature for me and my highest good.

I have faith in Divine Order and know that You are always in the midst of every situation and that all is well.

Thank you, dear God. And so it is.

Amen

Help me to release, Oh God, all anger, resentment, criticism or judgment against myself or others. Remove any hesitation from my heart to release my brothers and sisters from the bonds of unforgiveness. Let me see their innocence and shine the light of love upon them. I forgive all hurts, present or past, and enjoy the sweet relief of letting go of anything great or small that prevents me from moving beyond my own hurt feelings. Forgive me for any pain I have caused, great or small, to anyone and may they enjoy the sweet release from my own unforgiveness. I thank you for always seeing the best in me and never letting me forget that You love me no matter what. I am so grateful.

Amen

Dear God,

Allow me to see past this hurtful situation that I may be joined in Holy Union with this brother or sister. Remind me that we are both Your children and related in Spirit. As I surrender my need to be right, clear the way for Joy to take place and a new relationship to form out of the ashes of this difficult encounter. I am willing to be changed at depth, so that we both may be released by my awarness of the divinity with each of us. I am open and receptive to Your support and guidance in making this happen. Thanking you in advance.

Amen

Holy Spirit,

Come into my heart and fill it with the flow of loving forgiveness. Pour into me gratitude for this brother/sister, who stands before me crying for love. I behold his/her innocence and, in doing so, I behold my own. In their eyes I discover my own divinity and I return this gift to them. I offer my love in spite of any doubt, fear, judgment or criticism that may arise. I remind myself that my soul calls out through them for healing and I answer with compassion. Thank you for the opportunity this brother/sister brings to me to set us free and give room for my soul's growth. I am truly grateful.

Amen

Father-Mother God,

Forgive me for the harsh words I have spoken this day. Comfort me in my anguish over the hurt they caused to my brothers and sisters. Help me to watch over my tongue and guard my thoughts, so I may more easily catch anything that is not of love before it is expressed. I need Your loving support, as I come to more fully understand my relationship to Your other children. I am willing to learn and to grow. I surrender to the process now.

Amen

Lord, forgive me for those times when I speak without thinking and hurt others by my words. Teach me to be considerate in my ways so that I can be the light of love and compassion for everyone everywhere. Show me the way to be of service and support to Your vision for the world.

Amen

"All that I am and ever hope to be, I owe it all to Thee." I hold these words in my heart and mind this week wherever I go and whatever I do, regardless of how the days flow and situations go. Surrendering to the Eternal Love that lives within me and the Infinite Wisdom that guides me, I am becoming in each moment all that You have created me to be and that is all that I truly desire. Thank you so much.

Amen

My God, My Source, My Life,

I open my mind to Your wisdom that I may know what You would have me do. I open my being to Your direction that I may know where You would have me go. I open my heart to Your love that I may know what You would have me say and to whom. As I begin and end this day, my greatest desire is to serve You, Lord. Use me.

Amen

Dear God,

Today You have given me a brand new page to write a new story and the opportunity to tear up my old story. I am grateful for this new life, new light and new possibilities that open for me as I let go of the past and step into the Now. Teach me how to use these pages to create a life that is totally in alignment with Your Will and not my little ego will. I thank you in advance for a phenomenal life!

Amen.

Father-Mother God,

Walk with me this week and make my path straight and free from impediments and distractions. Give me the strength to look only to You regardless of what is standing before me. My Intention is to live fully as the expression of Your love, compassion, healing, abundance and peace. I surrender to Your guidance step by step. Lead me, Oh God, and I will follow.

Amen.

Lord of my Being,

If there is something I am meant to do, show me; if there is anything You want me to know, tell me; if there is someplace I am meant to be, take me there; and if there is an emptiness anywhere within my life, fill it with You. There is only one path I wish to take and that is the one leading me directly to You. In all that I say, all that I do and all that I am, God I want to know You more.

Amen.

Dear Lord,

How perfect is Your purpose for my life. Guide me toward fulfilling it so that I may go where You want me to go, do what You want me to do, and say what You want me to say to those whom You want me to say it, so that my mission here is complete and Your Will is done.

Amen.

Beloved Mother-Father God,

May I continually feel Your Divine Presence moving in and through me and through my body of affairs each and every moment of each and every day so that I am aligned with the purpose for which I came into existence.

Amen

Father-Mother God,

Help me stop today to smell the roses, to experience the moments of my day where I miss the greatest blessing: My connection with You.

Amen

My God,

Teach us how to let go of those things that no longer serve us. Help us release what must be removed for our highest good. In the midst of the sadness and desolation, comfort us but renew our faith that the light continues to shine in the darkness. Give us wisdom to know and follow the Truth.

Amen

Dear Lord,

Sometimes there are changes we can easily embrace and at other times there are changes that call us to move beyond our fears, doubts, regrets and hurts, and flow with the movement of Spirit as we are carried to a higher purpose. Help us break down our resistance and learn to embrace those changes that are most difficult. With Your love, support and guidance we can not only overcome but rise up to the Christ that is resurrected within the transition we are facing. We are willing.

Amen

This week, Dear Lord, I have begun in struggle yet I know that together we can turn it around and have a "do-over." Help me to find my way back to the way that aligns with You. My only desire is to tap into the divine part of me that is constantly connected with You but sometimes I lose the connection. Come Holy Spirit and jump-start my light that it may shine brightly to light the way back to the calm peace of my soul. I surrender.

Amen

My God, My Friend, My Helper, My Healer,

I give my life into Your care and keeping. There is only one prayer that escapes my lips each day: "God, I want to know You more." Let me know Your love when I am feeling unloved; help me feel Your strength in my weakest moments; fill me with Your courage when fear comes upon me; and, through all of the challenges I may face, allow me to see that You are always a driving force in leading me to my power and my true self. I give my life into Your care and keeping.

Amen.

Dear Lord,

May I stay focused on what is Truth beyond what I am seeing and feeling. Will You help me see that You are my only Source? Let me know that You are real in my life by putting up little signs along the way. I want to know You more. I want Your constant guidance and support. Be with me. Stay near.

Amen

God,

I place these days in Your hands to lead me in whatever way You see me fulfilling the purpose for which I came into the world. Whatever I may face, I am encouraged because I face it with You. I cannot fail with You by my side. You are my salvation. Send Your light to inspire me and restore me to the way I was with You before the world was.

Amen

Divine Spirit,

Bless the minutes of this day so my hours are filled with peace, joy, love and hope. Place more peace upon my heart so I offer peace in my words and actions. Give me more joy so I can spread it wherever I go and leave people feeling better. Fill me with more love so those who have never felt its comfort will know it through me. Expand my own capacity for hope so I am able to inspire within others the possibility of a better tomorrow. I want to be a channel for You every minute of this day and every day to come. Teach me Your ways so I may guide others. My only desire is to know You more, Divine Spirit, and to serve You in the building of Your Kingdom on Earth. Use me.

Amen

Lord,

You are my way, my truth and my light. Show me the way today to navigate the challenges and conditions that blocked my path and keep me from my true purpose, which is to do Your will and serve humanity. Help me to see beyond these challenges and conditions to the perfect truth that stands under all. Shine Your light upon them, so I am able to see my way clear. Bless those who are also finding their way, and if I can be of support in their process tell me what I need to know so that I can. Bless those who do not know You and let me be a shining demonstration in their eyes as to the wonderworking power of Your grace and majesty. If I falter in my step today, dear Lord, forgive me and lift me up so that I can begin again. In everything I do today, and in all my experiences, I want to know You more. Thank you for Your loving kindness and Your constant support.

Amen

My God, My Friend,

Walk with me today and all week and help me remember that You are there. Fill my days with peace, joy, love, good health and harmonious relationships. Help me to watch my words, give me power over my emotions and teach me to love when it is difficult. Open my heart to have compassion for those who are suffering and give me the strength to forgive those who hurt me. Show me how to live so closely aligned with Your Will that the world is a better place because I am in it. Remind me that in every moment I am co-creating my life and affecting the well-being of the planet. Bless my daily walk with You. Thank you so much.

Amen

Lord of My Being,

Today I live as You would have me live. Guide me every step of the way. Let me see You, let me feel You, let me know that You are there. I will look for You in everyone and everything and I will refuse to see anything else. Support me if I stumble and forgive my errors. Regardless of how well I do, Dear Lord, I am willing.

Amen

Father-Mother God,

There is so much to do today and I am feeling a bit overwhelmed. I know that, with Your guidance and support I am greater and stronger and more capable than I could be on my own; so I sincerely ask for Your added strength and stamina to accomplish what needs to be done today. Lead me, guide me and direct my activities so they run smoothly and efficiently. Show me how I can be most effective, what I can do and what I can release. If I should fall short of my human expectations, just let me live up to Yours. I am willing to let You be in charge because You do a much better job than I. Bless my mind, bless my body and bless my spirit. Thank you in advance for an absolutely awesome day!

Amen

Lord,

I surrender. Whatever is meant to be today, I let it be and help me to see the perfection in it. Whether I am at my job, in my home or driving in traffic, I surrender my judgment, condemnation, anger, guilt and fear. In Your Grace is the love I desire and the answer to my every concern. I face this day with no concerns because You are in the driver's seat steering the course of this day, and I am grateful.

Amen

Father-Mother God,

I awaken to a new world, a new energy and new possibilities. I am alive to the power of the Christ within me. I am alert to my thoughts and feelings that are out of alignment with the Christ of my being. I am awake to my connection with all life, accepting my responsibility for what I create. I am enthusiastic about life and about what You have in store for me this day. Lead, guide and direct me that I may do Your will. I am so grateful.

Amen

Dear Lord,

If there is anything that keeps me from being completely connected to You, I ask that You show me how to heal it. My greatest desire is to walk with You, talk with You and know that I am Your own Beloved Child. Let me feel You today and every day of this week in a deeper way than I have before. Reach deeply into my heart and touch the core of me, releasing all the hurt and pain I may be holding there so I can experience Your love and express it as You would. If I must experience any adversity today, give me what I need in order to face it with faith and a willingness to see what I need to see and learn what I need to learn. I love You, Lord, and I offer all that I am to You. Bless me, bless my family and friends, bless my co-workers and associates, bless this country and bless this world.

Amen

Father-Mother God,

As I move through this day strengthen my resolve to be the Child of God You created me to be. Let me so live my life that it becomes a testimony to how a life can be when it is lived in concert with You. Allow my choices to be thoughtful, considerate and in alignment with universal law and what is not simply what I want but what is good for all humanity. Show me where to walk so I can be right where I am needed right when I need to be there. Give me the words to speak that open hearts to feel the love streaming from you constantly. Teach me how to be Your truth teacher for the healing of the planet. I will walk today where the Christ of my being would walk and bring the light where there is darkness if You will guide me. I offer myself to You. Here I am Lord . . . Use me.

Amen

Dear Lord,

Sometimes it is difficult to motivate myself to do what I know needs doing, but Your ever-present love and light inspires me to move beyond my own doubts or lethargy and step into the innate power and magnificence You breathed into me at the moment of creation. Never let me forget that. Enlighten me to Your ways and guide me to be the very best me that I can be. Let Your validation be the only assurance that I need to know that I am created in Your image and am empowered to create the life I wish to live into. I surrender.

Amen

Precious Lord,

Open my eyes so that I see a world that is beautiful and perfect as You created it; open my heart so I can love this world as You love it; open my mind so my thoughts are of love, beauty and compassion; and open my mouth so I speak with the tongues of angels and offer words of kindness and support every moment of every day. Remind me that no matter what challenges arise this day, You and I together can face them and thrive. I am at Your service.

Amen

Holy Spirit,

Walk with me today and guide my every decision so I am living according to God's Will for me. Sometimes I miss a step but You always get me back on track. There are times when I am ready to give up because it just takes too much effort to go any further, but You encourage me to hang in there despite what is going on in my life. It is the love that surrounds me, the wisdom that guides me and the support that sustains me that makes it possible to make it through. Thank you from the depths of my heart that, if I know nothing else, You will never give me more than I can handle and You will always be there for me. I am so grateful.

Amen

My God, Jehovah, Yahweh,

Strengthen me today as I continue to make the effort to love and forgive, to stand in the face of the onslaught of fear and evil that is taking hold of my brothers and sisters around the nation. Help me to dig deep within me to find and release any anger, hatred, fear or evil that may be within me and contributing to the collective consciousness, so I can be a positive factor in healing this situation. Forgive me for all of those thoughts of hatred, anger and fear that I have held at any time in the past and support me in refraining from those thoughts in the future. I will work consciously today to be aware of who I am in this world and strive to be a better person for the emergence of a better world. I am so grateful that I have You, the Holy Spirit and all of the angels and archangels to support me. Thank you so much.

Amen

Dear Lord,

I pray that I have helped somebody this week; that I have been an inspiration in the midst of some despair; that I have brought the light to a dark place; and that I have given love where there was a need for it. Thank you for giving me opportunities to serve You, and if I happened to miss any please forgive me. Continue to lead, guide and direct me so that I am an instrument of Your love, light and inspiration everywhere I go and in everything I do. Bless me.

Amen

God,

Today I declare as the greatest day ever! As I walk through it, I am willing to see it that way despite what my eyes, my ears and my mind show me. I will see joy where there is sadness, love where there is hate, courage where there is fear and light where there is darkness. I will move beyond what my ego would desire and connect with Your Will. Support me in remembering my intention and help me love myself when I fall short. My only desire is to see the world as You see it and lovingly accept what is as is. Help me.

Amen

Holy Spirit,

Lead, Guide and Direct my way this day and every day so that I may fulfill my divine purpose for being here now. What would You have me do? Direct me to the work that is mine to do in supporting the awakening of humanity and the healing of the planet. Where would You have me go? Lead me to those places where I am called to do what You have willed for me. What would You have me say, and to whom? Guide my tongue and shape my words to carry love, comfort, possibility and hope to all those I encounter. By the power of Your Spirit, strengthen me so that I have what it takes to carry out what You have set before me. I am willing. I go to meet this day expectantly. Thank you for your constant support.

Amen

Lord of my Being,

I am so grateful for this day. As I move through it, let me feel Your presence each and every moment. God, I want to know You more. To know Your Will, that I may fulfill the purpose you have given me; to know Your Love, that I may love fully and unconditionally; to know Your Wisdom, that I may know what is mine to do and gain deeper insights for myself and others; to know Your Light, that I may share it with the world. In all things and in all ways, God I want to know You more.

Amen

Infinite Presence of Light and Love,

As You create my day, allow me to be a channel for Your power and magnificence and to see the light of your truth shining in and upon everything. Whether this is a day that flows peacefully and easily or a day challenged by conditions and circumstances, help me to see only what is Truth. In the midst of whatever occurs today, God I want to know You more. I go to meet this day filled with faith, hope and a willingness to see the perfection in everything. Thank you so much.

Amen

Holy Spirit,

Awaken in me today compassion and forgiveness in a powerful way. Allow me to accept what I experience as perfect in the spiritual sense. When I resist, strengthen my willingness. Give me the courage to face my deepest pain and greatest fears. If I can but touch the hem of the garment of wisdom and truth, clothing myself in peace, I know that I will thrive and bless those around me so that they too might thrive. I am willing. Help . . .

Amen

Dear God,

Today is Monday and You know what that is like for most of us. Although I would like to stay in bed and spend the day playing video games, I am willing to get up and see what this day is all about. But I will definitely need Your help. As I stand beneath the shower, remind me of the waters of life pouring through my very being at every moment cleansing, refreshing and restoring me in the face of and in the midst of whatever comes before me. As I eat my breakfast, remind me of the nurturing substance that infills and eternally surrounds me. As I drive to work, remind me that You are the driving force behind the flow of my life and encourage me to let You take the wheel. As I experience the content of my day, remind me that I am one with everyone and everything and that You have sent me nothing but angels to help me learn and grow on this soul journey. As I lay my head upon the pillow at the end of the day, remind me that it was whole and perfect as You created it regardless of what I created and what it looked like and felt like to me. I go forward now to meet this day with courage and faith, knowing that the Holy Spirit goes before me preparing my way for success.

Amen

Dear God,

As I begin the journey this day holds for me, stay close so I will know You are there. Even if I seem to pull away, reach out and pull me back to You. In my moments of mindlessness, place those billboards before me that remind me of Your eternal and all-encompassing Love. If I should fail to return love in the midst of what appears to be totally unlike love, forgive me and give Your love instead. What is Your will for me this day? That is my will also. Let me live this day in the fullness of the awareness of You in all that I do and in everyone I encounter. God, I want to know You more. I am so grateful.

Amen

Dear God,

Today it was difficult just getting out of bed. I did not feel like myself and I certainly did not feel like a Child of God. Yet, as I discovered that I was awake and breathing, it occurred to me that it was something to be grateful for. So I thank You. I thank You for waking me up this morning, for letting me see another day and giving me another opportunity to serve You. As I begin to walk through this day, lead guide and direct me so that I know what You will have me do, where You will have me go, what You will have me say and to whom. I am willing to take the risk of allowing You to create my day. I am willing . . .

Amen

Dear Lord,

As I move through this week let me not wander into overwhelm and lose sight of the beauty and love surrounding me. Guide me into more moments of reflection so I will not miss the little miracles that are a daily part of my life, but seem to fade in the face of a busy schedule. Help me to spend more time saying "I love you" to my family and friends and less time being too busy for them. Take the reins of my life so I can sit back and look out the window. Thank you for every moment that I am fully awake and conscious of my connection with You. I love you Lord.

Amen

Father-Mother God,

I pray for those whose hearts are heavy with anger, hatred, shame, fear and sadness. I pray that they realize the power of forgiveness and release to heal their hearts and relieve the burdens carried by their bodies. Give them the courage to create a space to allow others to be exactly who they are, letting go of all judgment, criticism and condemnation. Teach them that forgiveness is the gift they give themselves and a contribution to the healing of the planet.

Amen

Dear Lord,

I am willing to offer forgiveness to everyone who has ever harmed me and to myself for any harm I have ever done. Teach me to live in forgiveness and to be a catalyst for the healing of our world. Walk with me and guide me daily to know what You would have me do, where You would have me go, what You would have me say and to whom You would have me say it. I am willing to do your Will.

Amen

Today we seek the courage to look within and heal our pain. Though it is a scary process, we are willing to be healed. Guide us through those dark places where the shadows of our hidden selves reside. Shine the light of truth upon them and help us to see that what is there can no longer hurt us. With Your love and comfort, we are safe to move through the fire of the pain and come out on the other side totally unscathed and able to step forth into the life we wish to have. We forgive those who caused the pain, including ourselves and we put down the baggage of unforgiveness and resentment. We are free. Thank you, God.

Amen

Infinite Spirit,

Give me an understanding heart so that I have compassion for those who have created the circumstances in our world today. Let me show forgiveness toward them as You have shown forgiveness toward me for all my transgressions. Whatever the reasons for the way they have managed the affairs of governments near and far, help me to embrace their wounds as You have embraced mine and yet loved me anyway. Show me what is mine to do in the healing of this planet. Fill me with love so that I can love both friend and foe with equal measure. May Your will be done in me this day and every day to come. I surrender to Your guidance and Your wisdom, and I am willing to see the perfection in everything.

Amen

Lord,

I am grateful for the people who have harmed me in some way. I am grateful that they have been willing to bring up for me what was calling to be healed so that I am able to clear away any unhealed energy that has kept me stuck in being a victim. I am grateful that the experience of feeling the pain of betrayal has brought clarity and the peace that follows. I am grateful for the person I have become as a result of the process of healing and I thank them for being my healing angel so I am now able to open a channel for the light to enter in and make me whole. I offer forgiveness, love and a willingness to see that everything was perfect in the realm of divine truth. Thank you so much for these angels. I am truly grateful.

Amen

Gratitude

In everything give thanks, for this is the will of God in Christ Jesus concerning you.[96]

Although this is not one of the prayer categories used by Silent Unity in its ministry, prayers of gratitude are considered by those who have studied the effectiveness of prayer as the most powerful form of prayer.

Prayers of gratitude affirm our appreciation for what we already have, regardless of whether we perceive it as good or bad, and open the way for good beyond our ability to perceive this flow into our lives. When we are grateful for even our challenges, understanding they only serve to strengthen us and provide us with opportunities for spiritual growth, we are seeing everything as good and our consciousness is aligned with the energy of good; therefore, we attract "good" into our lives. Many people even keep gratitude journals as a way of affirming the ever-present goodness of God.

When we pray a prayer of Gratitude, we open a channel for the flow of good in our lives now.

---

[96] 1 Thessalonians 5:18 MKJV

Lord,

"How beautiful are Your dwelling places."

I know that You dwell not out there but in here within me and within all of my brothers and sisters everywhere. How beautiful are those in whom You dwell regardless of race, color, creed, religious belief, political affiliation or sexual orientation. I love and embrace all of Your children and work tirelessly to free myself from judgment of them or their behavior. I accept my purpose to simply love and serve humanity in all its forms. As I accept myself, Dear Lord, I am more open and receptive to accepting others. Thank you for loving me with all my faults and flaws so that I am compassionately achored in loving everyone else. I am so grateful for Jesus the Christ, our Brother, Way Shower and Master Teacher, for teaching us what love means. Thank you so much for so much.

Amen

Dear God,

Thank you for waking me up this morning, allowing me to see another day and providing me with one more opportunity to participate in building the Kingdom of Heaven on earth. Thank you for my challenges and adversities because they help me strengthen my God-Muscle and help shape me in your Image. Thank you for my blessings because they remind me of why the challenges and adversities were necessary. I am so grateful to know myself through Your vision and I am willing to see the perfection in everything— even when I can't. Thank you, Dear God.

Amen

God of All,

Teach me Your way so I am always following after You. Plant me where You want me to grow and I will send my branches out to carry the fruit of Truth. From this day forward I just want to be Your servant to do Your Will and carry Your Word in all that I am and in all that I do. Use me Lord.

Amen

Dear Lord,

You are my strength, my shield and my ever-present compass. You shore me up when life seems to weigh me down. You protect me from those who wish harm upon me. You lead, guide and direct me through the twists and turns of life and over the treacherous places to where You would have me be. I am so grateful for this unconditional love and support that I can depend upon no matter what. Thank you, God.

Thank you, Dear God, for the courage to face my fears, the strength to stand strong in the face of them and the power to build a divine outcome from the gifts I take from them. You have always been my way, my truth and my light and I am grateful.

Amen.

Lord God Almighty,

I am strengthened by knowing that You are here within me, as me, of me, and through me, from the moment I open my eyes each morning until I close them at night and throughout the hours that I sleep. I can walk through the day with confidence that You guide my every step, and I can sleep through the night with blessed assurance that You watch over me. If You are with me then nothing can harm me and no challenge can come upon me that together we cannot handle. Thank you for being my one constant in an ever-changing world. I am truly grateful.

Amen.

Dear God, My Healer and My Life-Giver,

I delight in a new day walking hand in hand with You and taking my light into the world to fulfill Your purpose for me. My heart overflows with love for You and its every beat reminds me that You are the guiding presence in my life. I eagerly step into this day, looking forward to sharing this overwhelming love, peace, joy and abundance with everyone I encounter—even the tailgaters, aggressive drivers and grumpy cashiers. You are the air I breathe and with each breath today I inhale the very essence of Your being, filling me with the power of the Christ and lifting me out of any condition or circumstance to see the wonder-working power of your grace. Oh, thank you Dear God; thank you for always being the constant in my life when others fail or disappoint me. Thank you for never judging me, even when I judge others. Thank you for your healing touch in those feverish times that come upon me. Thank you for giving me all that I need to do all that I need to do. I really love you.

Amen

My God,

I am grateful for this week of thanks-giving for it brings together millions of hearts being thankful together and raises the vibration for the world. Helps us to continue living with an attitude of gratitude and give thanks every day of the year for everything. Remind me that everything is good and worthy of gratitude, no matter how it shows up in my life. As I begin this day, I am grateful for another day and another opportunity. I am so grateful to know You in my life and to feel Your presence within me. Thank you, thank you, thank you.

Amen

Beloved God,

Thank you on this day when so many are taking the time to give thanks where friends and family are gathering to share in your magnificent bounty and remembering so many who have gone before us. I am so grateful for my life and for the family with whom I chose to enjoy this experience and to love, and also for the friends who have chosen to love me. I am grateful for the food, the laughter and the joy we will share today and always. May I continue to be worthy of the wonderful people You have brought me. Thank you for my children, who have brought both tears and laughter along the way but I wouldn't trade it for anything in the world. Thank you for everything in my life. All of it is so good because You make it so. Thank you. I am truly grateful.

Amen

Dear Lord,

This week, as I move toward the day of Thanksgiving, I set my intention to have an attitude of gratitude each and every moment of each and every day. I am willing to be grateful for whatever is before me by seeing the perfection in everything. Today, I am grateful for my challenges. I know that my challenges are not there to harm me or break me down, but to strengthen me and lift me up into my true power. As I am compelled to become a greater person than I was before the challenge came, in order to rise above it, I am forever changed and move forward into my life with renewed courage, deeper insights and a closer connection with the divinity within me. I realize that You never give me more than I can handle and You always give me all that I need to do all that I need to do. I am grateful for my challenges and I go forward to meet them with the same enthusiasm that I go to meet my blessings. Thank you so much, Dear Lord. I am grateful.

Amen

My God,

What a wonderful week this has been. Whether I experienced pain and suffering or joy and peace, I am willing to see the perfection in it all. As I rest from my labors, remind me to take a moment to breathe and take in the inspiring love that fills my very being and gives me the power to move toward another week with renewed purpose. I choose the power of peace in every moment and give up the struggle so that I may go with the flow of Your Divine Will for me. Thank you so much for all you do to make that possible.

Amen

Dear God,

As this breathtaking week comes to a close, I am simply but powerfully grateful—grateful for a new world awakening, where everyone of every race, color, creed and sexual orientation is truly my brother and sister, and where we are moving toward oneness with a new resolve and a new purpose. I rest from my work this week with a greater sense of peace and a bigger heart. Thank you for showing me that Your dream for us has been playing out all along. I am excited, expectant and filled with absolute joy. I can't wait to see what You have in store for us.

Amen

Heavenly Father,

I begin this week expectantly, looking forward with enthusiasm and excitement to what wonders You have in store for me. Whether I experience it as good, bad or indifferent, it is all good because everything is always preparing me to move ever closer to You and Your will for me. As You created the world and named it "good," I name everything in my life "good." I trust in Your love and Your grace, knowing that I am your beloved child in whom You are well pleased; and, as such, You would never lead me through anything I cannot handle and that is not for my highest good. So I thank you in advance for the wonderful outworking of my life and I go to meet it with faith and courage.

Amen

My God,

I admit that, by myself, I can do nothing. All that I am or ever hope to be rests with You. You are the strength that shores up my weakness; You are the courage that dispels my fears; You are the companion that eliminates my loneliness; You are the wisdom that relieves my doubt; and You are the light keeps the darkness away. With Your ever-present love and support, my power and magnificence shines forth in an awesome way. I surrender this day into Your care and keeping and I step forward without a care in the world. I love You so much. Thank you for everything.

Amen

Wonderful, Wonderful Spirit,

How precious are these moments when I take the time to get in touch with You and that Divine part of me. I am grateful for the tender embrace of Your eternal love. I begin my walk this day wrapped in the assurance that You continually support, provide and guide me. With this knowing I cannot fail. I surrender my will to Your Will. May I see Your hand in everything that arises today and may I see You in every face I look upon. Today is going to be a great day because You are in it. Thanks a bunch!

Amen

Dear Lord,

In all Your ways and all my days You fortify and sustain me. You provide for me in the midst of what appears to be an economic crisis. You fill me with peace where there is the evidence of war. You lift me up when outside circumstances would tear me down. You are my way, my Truth and my light that guides my every step. There is no other joy than the joy I feel when I am consciously in your presence. My only prayer request today is "God I want to know You more."

Amen

God,

You have been my constant companion through this week, giving me strength and courage, peace and unconditional love. You have loved me so that I was able to love my sister or brother when they were being unloveable. You have kept me from losing my temper every time I was tempted to do so and You have helped me keep my mouth shut when I wanted to say something so badly. You have been my shelter in this storm of world crisis. As I start this weekend, help me take care of myself to renew and revitalize in preparation for another week. Keep my focus on You and not the headlines. Show me ways to find joy for myself and to share joy with others. I am looking forward to these days of relaxation and I am grateful. Thank you so much.

Amen

Mother-Father God,

You have given me so much to do that I sometimes feel inadequate to live up to your expectations; yet, when I look back at my life and all that I have accomplished, I know that with the assignment comes all of the attributes and abilities required to carry it out successfully. I offer myself in service to You and all of my sisters and brothers willingly and with great humility. I am strengthened by your expectations, because if You expect it I am more than capable of it. Thank you for those whom you have entrusted to my care for healing and support. Thank you for those into whose care You have entrusted my healing and support. I love you truly, dear God. Thank you. Thank you. Thank you.

Amen

My God, My Comforter, My Deliverer, My Protector,

You comfort me when grief and sadness overtake my mind and body; You deliver me from the traps and pitfalls of my own egoic self; and You protect me from the onslaught of my negative thoughts and emotions. Your eternal love and great mercy pursues my every step and I am wrapped in the powerful garment of your wisdom and guidance. Today, as I allow You to create the greatest good for my life, joy bubbles up in my heart and I know that all is well. Whatever comes, whatever doesn't work out quite like I expect it, whatever happens that brings up my own stuff, it will not matter because my Comforter, My Deliverer, My Protector, My God will take care of me and all is Swell. Thank you so much for the greatest day of my life.

Amen

General

And all things, whatsoever ye shall ask in prayer, believing, ye shall receive.[97]

A general prayer may be used when we are having a difficult time deciding what to pray for or how to even pray in light of what is occurring at the moment.

When we pray a general prayer, we are seeking the absolute perfection in us, in others and in every situation, condition or circumstance that appears to have caused a disruption in the perfect pattern of the cosmic consciousness.

This type of prayer brings us back into alignment with the truth of our being, renews our mind and transforms the situation. We are in quest of a new way of looking at the situation, so that we see our way clear to God's guidance and direction.

---

[97] Matthew 21:22 KJVA

Dearest God, both Father and Mother of us all,

We consciously connect with that loving energy from which we were expressed and open ourselves to all its glory; that our hearts may be expanded and our territories enlarged to encompass *every* part and particle of Your creations.

May we be ever mindful of Your love as we come into contact with our brothers and sisters, so that all our thoughts, words and actions convey the healing, harmonizing and Holy Spirit power of Love.

May we know no anger, hatred or vengeance toward anyone. May we have the courage to give love in the face of anything not of love. May we see that blessed divinity within everyone and act according to the Truth that we know of their Being. May we create, through loving vision, a world where love has no opposites and no boundaries.

We acknowledge the beloved brothers and sisters of African descent who courageously endured the error thinking of humankind and left a legacy of strength, beauty, power, pride and dignity.

We acknowledge their descendents who have survived to live out the dreams of their ancestors. We acknowledge all our brothers and sisters of every nation, culture, color, creed, sexual orientation and religious choice.

From the Love that is our Divine Self, we love our World without boundaries. And so it is.

Amen.

Father-Mother God,

How wonderful is this season of joy, hope and rebirth, when I honor the birth of the Blessed Jesus and celebrate the Christ being born anew in me. As I view the holiday lights, remind me that the light shines within me and is my way out of the darkness. As I observe the holiday decorations, remind me of the beauty within me that shows through if I let my light shine out into the world. As I listen to the familiar carols, remind me that the song of God is eternally singing through me when I raise my voice to express love and peace to everyone. As I come together with family and friends to share meals, gifts and holiday traditions, remind me that I am part of the family of the world forever connected, and that I am here to love everyone, everywhere, whether I agree with them or not. Thank you for the powerful demonstration for the world that came with the birth of Jesus the Christ. Thank you for the Christ Light that is reborn in me each day. I open myself to receive it and I am willing to share it. Keep us safe, peaceful and comforted. Happy Birthday Jesus.

Amen

God,

Help me to swim through the turbulent waters of my life like a fish, climb over the mountains of my mortal errors like the mountain lion and fly above those things that would pull me down into the depths of despair like the Eagle.

Amen.

Dear God,

Free me from the grip of fear, anger, doubt, and despair as I daily face a world in chaos. Keep my heart open to feel your love no matter what I'm seeing with my human eyes. As others get caught up in this energy of lack, loss and violence, help me stay focused on the promise You have made that You will never leave me comfortless. If I should forget, Dear God, send a loving angel to help me remember who I am and then allow me to help others to do the same. This week I am committed to letting my light shine in celebration of the "Light of the World" that came forth in Bethlehem thousands of years ago. May I remember that this light still shines in the midst of the seeming darkness. Be my guide, be my truth and be my way.

Amen

My Friend, My God,

What a week this has been. I have seen the state of our country continue to decline and I have heard the cries of millions, but I know, beyond a shadow of a doubt, that a better day is coming. I put my trust in you no matter what. I will go forward and see what the end will be, with great expectations and hope in my heart. And thank God it's Friday!

Amen

You Who Are My True Beloved,

How lovely is the dwelling place within the comfort and safety of Your ever-abiding love. Let me fall into that place today where nothing can disturb the calm peace of my soul. My desire is to live totally in the ecstasy of quiet certitude—the knowing that all is well, even within the midst of overwhelming chaos. I will look to the eye of the storm and see beyond what my human eyes deceive and find the perfect light of hope shining brightly, lighting my way. I walk today where the Christ walks and feel Your presence there. So sweet is this . . .

Amen

Dear God,

Bless those who whose hatred and racism toward those who do not look like them are rising to the surface in the face of their fears and insecurities. They, too, are my brothers and sisters and I pray the opening of their hearts to accept all brothers and sisters of every race, color, creed, religion and sexual preference. Awaken them to the truth of their being as one with You and every living thing upon this planet. May they realize that below the surface of the very thing that causes them to feel separate from the rest of your children, is the one thing that joins us all and erases the outer differences. Help them to feel Your love flowing from their hearts and coursing through their veins, a love that knows no differences—only sameness. My love and my heart go out to them. I cannot hate them back. They are my brothers. If only they could see how much I love them. Let them see, Dear God, let them see. Thank you very much.

Amen

God of My Being,

On this very first day of a new week in which everything is uncertain and we're dancing on the edge of chaos, my sincerest and only prayer is: GOD, I WANT TO KNOW YOU MORE!

Amen

Dear Lord,

I pray today for those who are unable to pray for themselves; those whose hearts are heavy and bodies are weary, who have given up on life and given up on You. I pray that they find that loving place inside of them that connects them with You, to discover that when it appeared no one was there You were right there all the time waiting for the call. Bring them a tiny spark of light that opens a small crack in their pain for a ray of hope to slip in. Lift them up and help them stand, Dear Lord, to walk into Your love and find their way again. Today, I pray for those who cannot pray for themselves.

Amen

Amazing God,

I am so blessed today to be alive to witness Your amazing grace and feel a new energy of oneness, hope and possibility that is resonating across these United States and across the globe. Thank you for our new President-Elect and his family. May they continue to surrender to your guidance and direction; and may their faith be strengthened as they go to meet a destiny like no other before. I am proud to be an American, but I am prouder to be a child of God. Thank you, Dear God.

Amen

Dear God,

Today is Friday. Yay! Today is also Halloween. As I complete this week, I set my intention to allow myself to take my cue from the children. I will rediscover the wonder of my own being. I will give myself permission to act silly and have fun. I will look around me at my world as if it were the first time. I will let myself look foolish and not care how I look to others. I will play nice with the other kids and not let myself be bullied. I will ask for comfort when I get a boo-boo and not be ashamed to cry. I will be happy regardless of what is going on around me and I will snuggle up in my bed at night without a care in the world. Thank you for giving me back my innocence. Have a nice weekend, God.

Amen

Dear Lord,

As we prepare to celebrate Mothers and the loving, nurturing, and supportive spirit they represent, teach us how to love, nurture and support ourselves by allowing the Divine Feminine energy of the Holy Spirit to actively live with us as the one true Mother. May we allow Her love to permeate and transmute our fears, our doubts and our suffering into the power of God's Eternal Light of Love. For this and so much more, we are truly grateful.

Amen

Sheila Gautreaux

Father-Mother God,

Bless this day when we exercise our rights as citizens, equal under the laws of the constitution, to choose those whom we would have lead us in the coming years. Give us the courage of our beliefs and help us to see beyond our prejudices, biases, criticism, condemnation and judgments to the divine truth that underlies this entire process. Lead, guide and direct our choices from the depths of our being that we might create a world that works for all. Protect our candidates and, above all, protect the clauses of the Constitution upon which this nation was built. Remind us that absolutely every one of us is Your beloved son or daughter in whom You are well pleased. Helps us to realize that we are all connected, and that every word, every thought, and every action impacts not merely, the few but all. I pray this day for Barack Obama and his family, John McCain and his family, Joe Biden and his family and Sarah Palin and her family. I ask that the hearts of those who are carrying hatred, prejudice, resentment and plans for revenge, attack or retaliation, be softened so they know that no matter what the outcome, You are still in charge and that Your Will is being done this day. Thank you for your constant love and support. It is always so comforting to know that You are there.

Amen

My God,

In whom I live and move and have my being, bless me as You always bless me, and bless these last two days of this very significant election. Bless all of the candidates from local to nationwide and their families. Bless those who have been given the right to vote and those who have accepted that right. May we act as the symbol of justice and be blind to everything except what is truly important—the issues at hand and what is for the good of our nation and our world. Protect our presidential candidates and keep them safe. Forgive those whose thoughts are filled with doing them harm. Regardless of the outcome, dear Lord, it is and will be exactly what we need and what will elevate us to our highest and best. Bless this week for me and may I do Your will and see the perfection in everything. Thank you in advance for the greatest week ever.

Amen

Yahweh,

Breathe into me the breath of life; inspire and renew me. Illumine me and let my light shine; uplift me and guide me to uplift others. Revitalize and strengthen my resolve. Fill me with Your loving presence and grant me grace today and forever more.

Amen

My God,

I truly did not feel like getting up this morning, but Your welcoming love inspired me to open my eyes and see a beautiful morning, to open my mind to the infinite possibilities that await me and to open my heart to the joy that is available in every moment. I am so grateful for Your guidance. I go forward to meet this day with expectation and enthusiasm. Bless every person and situation today. Help me to remember that I am Your child, loved, adored, prospered, and that I am one with every man, woman and child and Mother Earth. May I live today as that truth. I am so very grateful.

Amen

Dear God,

How magnificent You are and how wonderful are Your works. I celebrate You in my heart and the spaces between my breaths. I am filled with joy because You love me. I dance delightfully because You take care of me. I sing to You in the notes of my music because You are my song and You light up my life. Let us play together this week and have fun.

Amen.

Dear Lord,

As I begin this weekend, I reflect on what has occurred since Monday and how I have served You in the world. Have I loved generously? Have I listened lovingly? Have I judged with compassion? Have I looked upon my brothers and sisters and seen The Christ light shining from their eyes? Have I played small or stepped beyond my comfort zone to be a messenger of hope and possibility? I pray that I have lived as a testament to Your unconditional love and mercy. If I have fallen short in any way, forgive and support me in loving myself anyway. As I renew and recharge this weekend, prepare me to take up the mantle and do an even better job next week. Have a great weekend God. See you in church.

Amen

Father-Mother God,

When I awoke this morning to the singing of the birds outside my window, I realized that, no matter what the appearance might be, this truly is a wonderful world. The song of the birds reminds me that there is always a song in our hearts if we are willing to hear it and stop to listen. The birds do not care about the economy or the bail-out, the stock market or the Presidential debate and its issues. The birds simply continue to sing their song in praise of You. Today, I will sing my song in the midst of despair and disappointment. I will sing my song when I am feeling like the victim. I will sing my song when the balance in my bank account is not enough to take care of what is required. I will sing my song when feeling lost and alone. I will continue to praise You with a song in my heart every moment of the day. Let my song rise to the heavens and join the angelic chorus to create a vibration so powerful that it reverberates throughout the earth. Today I sing God's praises and all is well.

Amen

Dear God,

As I begin this week free me from anything I have brought from last week and allow me to live each moment of this week as if it had no past. If I should happen to forget, gently remind me and help me love myself back into that moment.

Amen.

Dear God,

Okay, it's Monday again and ordinarily I would grumble about it and wish I could stay in bed but this is no ordinary day. It is a day of remembrance. Today I remember who I am, a child of God. I remember that I am blessed and I am a blessing. I remember that nothing outside of me can touch these truths. I also remember that my job, the paycheck, the stock market and my IRA are not the source of my supply. You are. I will walk through this day with my head held high, feeling my blessedness and moving forward with the assurance that you've got my back and everything's gonna be alright. I love you God and I love me from the top of my head to the bottom of my feet. And I am willing to see the perfection in everything that arises this day. And so it is.

Amen

Oh Lord,

Thank God it's Friday! I have loved my brother as myself, beheld the Christ in my sister, been willing to see the perfection in the situations and affirmed daily my beauty and magnificence. It has not been easy, but I have persevered. Now, I need a moment to just be angry, sad, annoyed and judgmental. I know that You will love me anyway and I know that through Your love I will love myself anyway. As I catch my breath this weekend, renew my strength and fortify my courage to continue to walk in love and compassion and carry the light of truth into the world. Bless me, bless my family and friends, bless the nation and bless the world. Thank you so much, Lord, and have a nice weekend.

Amen

Mother-Father God,

Touch my heart with peace and balance as I deal with a challenge today even before my morning coffee. Because You are the answer before the prayer has been spoken, I am assured that the solution has already been prepared. I will move forward with the confidence that a door has been opened that leads to my good and I will step through it poised and centered in my alignment with You at the center of my heart. There is no place where You are not. There is no situation that You have not already handled. There is no darkness where Your light shines and Your light shines everywhere. Today I am guided by Your light, I lean upon Your love, and I am strengthened.

Amen

Sheila Gautreaux

PRAYER FOR OUR PRESIDENT-ELECT

God, you have chosen this man Barack Obama to guide us through this era in these United States of America and we thank You. Now, he needs Your love, guidance and direction more than ever before. Keep close watch over him. Comfort him when he gets discouraged. Carry him when his load gets too heavy. Refresh and revitalize him when he gets weary. Surround him with Your angels and archangels, so that "not even his foot may dash against the stone." Stand with him and fortify him when he must face our enemies, but allow him to face them with love and remember that they are also Your children. When he has a tough decision to make, popular or not, give him the courage to do what he knows is right and for the good of the many. Bless him, bless his family. Keep them safe and regardless of what is going on in the White House or in the World, let them continue to experience joy. Thank you for the hope that is tangible, the possibility that is palpable and the bright future that is evident.

Amen

Father-Mother God,

In whom we live and move and have our being, we make a conscious decision right now to surrender to Your will and release the selfish desires of our human will, that we may live eternally in the Kingdom of Heaven on earth. We value Your love and your bountiful blessings, and we offer ourselves to the experience of them from this day forward.

We release the tendency to judge, condemn and make guilty our brothers and sisters; instead, we look upon them with the same vision You hold for them. We see them guiltless, sinless, innocent and perfect as you created them. We extend our open heart to all of Your creation and lovingly and unconditionally embrace all. We offer them love to replace hate, joy to replace sadness, assurance to replace doubt, courage to replace fear, peace to replace anger, compassion to replace thoughtlessness and abundance to replace lack. We choose this day to serve You by serving humanity and to worship at the altar of love.

As we go about the work of Spirit, we remain open and receptive to being reminded of our commitment to Your will and to our responsibility for carrying the light of the world within us to guide the way for all of humanity.

We are truly grateful that You always hear us and knowing, even before we ask, that our prayers are answered. In the manner of our elder brother, Jesus Christ, we will do Your Will. And so it is. So be it.

Amen.

Divine Creator,

In which we live and move and have our being, we celebrate our oneness with You this day and in every moment throughout this day. While we honor those individuals who have worked toward independence and those who have given their lives for independence, we honor first and foremost our interdependence with You. We willingly surrender our own little will to be embraced and guided by Your greater will for our lives.

In our forgetting, remind us that in Your care and keeping we are always clothed in love and housed in grace. By Your loving hand we are fed with the fruits of Spirit and filled with the sweetness of eternal life. Through Your eyes we see ourselves as your perfect creations, adorned in beauty and splendor, radiant and divine. We are the notes upon Your composition and the brush strokes upon Your canvas. In our dependence upon You is our joy made complete.

We are eternally grateful that we need never be unlinked from the golden chord that connects us to Your womb. Give us this day all that we require to live a joyous life in Your kingdom. We are willing to receive it. To this we say . . .

Amen.

Divine Light of Wisdom,

We call forth the Holy Spirit to come into our presence and make itself known to us that we may experience the fullness of Being. We welcome the flow of consciousness that moves across the universe and permeates all existence to pour itself into us and fill us with the sweet ecstasy and total joy that comes from our true nature.

We see with our "Simple Eye" the beauty of our brothers and sisters and all of creation and we allow the illusions of judgment and condemnation to recede back into the nothingness from whence they came.

We hear the harmonics of the universe playing gently upon our "Simple Ear" straight through the muddle of incongruent words of dissociation, disharmony and disunity that issue forth from our brothers and sisters as a result of the illusion of separation, and we know their oneness with us.

We embrace all humanity and all creation in the arms of love from our "Simple Heart" in spite of negative, offensive or unloving actions that appear to be real and recognize that every attack is a call for loving thoughts, loving words, and loving action.

We recognize that the time for awakening is now and we joyously rise to the call. We are willing to be the truth that we wish to see expressed in our world each and every moment of each and every day. We know that truth, we are that truth and we vow to live that truth right here and right now. So be it.

Amen.

Divine Spirit,

We hold in our hearts our brothers and sisters who left their physical bodies on September 11, 2000 and left us to grieve their transition. We will not forget them. We will not forget that they were important to us. We will not forget that all men and women are important to us. We will not forget that every living thing is important to us. We will make a conscious effort to memorialize them by loving God with all our minds, hearts and souls; loving every brother and sister as God loves them; and loving ourselves as we are loved by our God.

As our world struggles to find its way back to the path and our country seeks a way to forgive, release and let go of its anger, hatred and desire for retaliation, we hold in our hearts the vision of a New World Order—a world where all people *feel* safe, a world where no one is hungry, a world where all dis-ease of the body has been healed, a world where Mother Earth is honored and returned to her wholeness, a world where the environment has been restored to its original purity, and a world where all of us live in harmony and love.

We hold in our minds the vision of the Kingdom of Heaven here and now, where love, peace, joy, abundance and wholeness is the norm rather than the exception.

We believe this is possible and we invite the Holy Spirit to guide us in making it a reality in our consciousness and in our lives. We know that this is Your will for us and we will do Your will each and every moment of each and every day.

Thank you, Dear God. And so it is. And so it shall be.

Amen.

Divine Power of Unlimited Good,

We offer our gratitude for Your presence within us, through us and around us. We willingly join with You in this moment of Thanksgiving and acknowledge that You are our One True Source. We put aside our bequests and praise only You.

We thank You for each breath we take. We thank You for the water that flows from the mountaintop. We thank You for the ebb and flow of the tides. We thank You for the sacred dance of the sun and moon. We thank You for the cosmic choreography of the universe. We thank You for each birth and each death. We thank You for each smile and each tear. We thank You that we can feel pain, so that we may experience the joy that follows. We thank You for every situation that strengthens our connection with you. We thank You for love, life, laughter, prosperity, peace, health and joy. We thank you for everything.

Amen.

Sheila Gautreaux

Beloved Father-Mother God,

We awaken the power of the Christ within us as we observe the birth of our elder brother, Jesus.

We call forth the quickening power of the Christ to infill us with love to be extended toward our brothers and sisters.

We align ourselves with the peace of the Christ to bring harmony to the planet and join together everyone regardless of race, color, religious beliefs, sexual orientation or political creeds.

We offer the gift of the Christ to everyone we meet and behold the divinity that is the true nature of their being.

We release the need for fear, worry, anxiety, doubt or lack and remember that you are the single Source of all our good and we trust in our relationship with you that is eternal rather than those things of the outer which are always changing and never reliable.

We sing the song of joy, peace, harmony and love and experience its vibration as it encircles the globe and permeates every heart.

We celebrate and honor our elder brother, Jesus the Christ, and thank Him for His loving gift to us all.

Amen.

Dear Lord,

We claim the power of light as it flows in, through and around us, knowing it is us. We align ourselves with the warmth of its flame to comfort us. We follow its radiance as it guides us. We embrace its power as it illumines us. We celebrate its beauty as it brings us joy and peace. We extend the light to our brothers and sisters everywhere as it extends itself to us. Through this love offering, we join in the at-one-ment and are lifted into the fullest expression of God, our Creator. We extend this light to cover the globe and span the universe, returning our consciousness to its rightful place in the All-ness of the All. By this Light we are made whole and by this wholeness salvation is accomplished. In gratitude, we acknowledge this Truth. So be it.

Amen.

Sheila Gautreaux

Dear God,

Let the words of my mouth and the meditations of my heart be acceptable to You and be a healing agent for the uplifting of all of my brothers and sisters everywhere and for every living, breathing thing upon the earth.

May I not stray into the temptation to seek that which fulfills me alone, but to desire with every fiber of my being the very best and the greatest for all Your creations.

Where I see a need, remind me of Your abundant good and teach me to see the fulfillment through Your power and Your love for us all.

When I encounter what may appear as attack, blaze through me the light of Your love and grace that I may express that love as Your gift through me.

And, God, open my eyes that I may see only love; open my ears that I may hear only love; open my mouth that I may speak only love; and open my heart that I may only love.

I am honored to be my Brothers' keeper and I accept my responsibility for the well-being of all humankind upon the planet.

I am willing to be Your vessel for love, that where I walk love goes before me, love follows me and love surrounds me.

Use me, God, use me to hear the call of my brothers and sisters to bring the chaos to a screeching halt and take the gentle ride to where love is willing to carry us all if we surrender.

I am eternally grateful to you, Dear God.

Amen

From *A Course in Miracles*:

Father, I thank You that Your promises will never fail in my experience, if I but test them out. Let me attempt therefore to try them, and to judge them not. Your Word is one with You. You give the means whereby conviction comes, and surety of Your abiding Love is gained at last. [98]

And Dear God,

We trust that which comes upon us, realizing that it comes from the Holy Spirit's desire to lead us home to you; and we lift our eyes to the hills, knowing our help comes from You. As the outer circumstances arise to threaten the calm peace of our souls, we stand upon Your promises and surrender to the Divine Plan You have mapped out for our lives that they may evolve into eternal life in the Kingdom of Heaven. We go to meet our tests with joy, knowing that with You we cannot fail.

Amen

---

[98] *A Course in Miracles* (CA: Fdn. For Inner Peace 1975, 1985, 1992), W-pII . . . 327.2:1.

For Our Loved Ones

For this reason we have always prayed for you, ever since we heard about you. We ask God to fill you with the knowledge of his will, with all the wisdom and understanding that his Spirit gives.[99]

Praying for others has a powerful healing effect upon our lives. By stepping outside of our own life and activities and offering the transforming power of prayer to someone else, the miracle occurs.

When we focus our attention on someone else's need, we have to forget about our own. In that ultimate act of unselfishness and concern for our brothers and sister, our stuff becomes what it is—empty and meaningless.

When we pray for others it is important to hold the vision of their perfection and place no emphasis upon the need, except for declaring it as we want to see it out-pictured in their lives.

As I tell my prayer students, if you cannot see beyond the situation when praying for someone else, don't pray. It is best to ask another person, who can hold the perfect vision of wholeness, to pray for them instead.

Prayers for our loved ones are especially powerful, because there is a strong element of love and a deep connection that is a microcosm of the love and connection we have with God and all of creation.

It is also easier to feel our prayers when praying for a loved one; however, it is also harder to detach from the situation or condition.

---

[99] Colossians 1:9 GNB

Mothers' prayers are the most powerful of all, because the connection to their children is still supported by the invisible umbilical chord, and is very similar to our connection with our Creator—God.

Today, Dear God, I am praying for my loved ones. Wherever they are and whatever their circumstances are, take care of them, surround them with Your love and shower them with Your grace. If they are close to You, draw them closer; if they are not, draw them even closer; and if they are troubled or in the midst of a great challenge, light their way and carry them through the dark times to the light. If they are dealing with a physical challenge, bless their minds so they realize that sickness is not the truth of them and bless their bodies so they are made whole. If they are off in a far country fighting a war or supporting a cause, keep them safe and fortify their courage, and bring them home walking on their own two feet. Bless my loved ones and remind them that they are truly loved and never alone.

Amen

Dear Lord,

My daughter is in the far country and cannot find her way home. Watch over her and keep her safe from harm. Guide her feet along the path that leads her home. If she should stumble, lift her up into your loving arms and hold her there until she is strong enough to continue her way. When the darkness comes, light the way for her to see that she is close to her journey's end. Dry her tears in the moments of sadness. Give her courage when fear overtakes her. Smooth the rough places and carry her over the mountains of challenge. When others turn against her, remind her that You are her champion. Cover her from the cold winds of adversity and free her from the chains of addiction. Whisper Your love in her ears when she feels alone and remind her that my love is waiting here to take her in.

To you, Oh Lord, I return your precious gift and know that only You can care for her better than I.

Thank you, Dear Lord.

Amen

Precious Lord,

Watch over my beloved son. He is adrift on turbulent seas. Enormous swells of adversity have overtaken him and he is about to drown in fear. Place Your hand upon his and help him steer a steady course. Guide him through the troubled waters of his life. Fill him with courage and faith when he loses his will to go on, and warm him with Your love when the chill winds of trouble blow. When the waves of guilt come upon on him, let him know that You have never held anything against him. When he becomes weary of heart, give him the strength to continue. Be the captain of his ship. Light the lamp in the lighthouse of the harbor of peace, so that he may realize that You are always there and find his way home again.

I will keep a light burning in my heart to lead him back to my love.

Thank you, Precious Lord.

Amen

Dear God,

Take care of my beloved husband, as he goes to work today. Guide him through the traffic of thoughts and help him find You. Be his hands, his voice, his eyes and his ears, so that he may be successful in every task he undertakes. Open his mind to the wisdom of the masters to receive an abundance of creative ideas for productive work. Make him a channel of love and compassion to lend a helping hand to those around him. When the pressures mount, give him peace; when his body tires, give him strength; when his mind is weary, fill him with inspiration; and when he feels he stands alone, tell him "I Am there." If he should lose this work that he loves, remind him that You are the source of all that he needs. And when the day has ended, and he hurries home again, take the wheel on the highway of life and return him safely to his family and to my loving arms and grateful heart. Thank you, Dear God.

Amen

Dearest God,

I am blessed by this loving person who is my girlfriend, and I thank You that she is in my life.

Her words of support lift my spirit when doubt makes me falter. Her generous words of praise fill me with esteem when insecurity blinds me to what is so good about me. Her strong shoulder and deep compassion comfort me when my heart is broken. Her tough love kicks me in the rear when I'm wallowing in despair. Her bright smile and hearty laugh bring me great joy when sadness covers me. Her tender touch strokes my fevered brow when my body seems to fail.

Oh, Dear God, I love this powerful woman who willingly shares herself with me and always reminds me that I am wonderful and that I am loved.

I am blessed by this loving person who is my girlfriend, and I thank You that she is in my life.

Amen

Dear God,

In Your light and wisdom lies the answer to why we lose the ones we love and the comfort for our grief. In the midst of our pain and tears we are made peaceful by Your presence. Surrendering our brother's spirit into Your hands we are comforted by the knowing that he has transfigured the limited vehicle of the human body and transitioned into his perfect state. We release this loving soul to go forward to meet his divine destiny.

Help us, his loved ones, to learn to live without his joy, his laughter and his loving nature. Remind us when loneliness overcomes us that he is always near, watching over us and keeping us surrounded by his love. Support us in keeping our memories of him within our hearts, that we may never forget what he contributed to our lives. Give us the words, actions and courage to support each other and be a light for all who are grieving this loss.

We trust in Your goodness and love, Dear Lord, and know that all is well with him and with us. For Your love and for the love that he exemplified, we thank You in the name and after the loving nature of our elder brother, Jesus the Christ.

Amen

PRAYER FOR OUR NATION & OUR WORLD

Dear Lord,

We are in the midst of great turmoil upon this planet. Our house is divided and the walls are crumbling. We are so caught up in fear and in being right, that we are so unhappy. We have placed all our trust in things that cannot help us and no longer serve us. We think we're alone and on our own. Right now, Dear Lord, send a gentle touch upon our hearts to remind us that no matter what is going on, You are still God and have this situation under control. Help us to be willing to see the perfection in all of this. Remind us that You are never more than a breath away. Guide us to a place of love and forgiveness and teach us to love ourselves when we fall short. We place this nation and the entire world in Your care and keeping. We bless every man, woman, child, animal, tree, plant and blade of grass. We bless our leaders. May they remember that, in their elected roles of responsibility, the good of the many outweigh the good of the few. Bless Barak Obama, John McCain, Joe Biden, Sarah Palin and their families. Regardless of whether we are for or against them as our candidates, they are Your sons and daughters in whom You are well pleased and, therefore, our brothers and sisters. Do not allow our political preferences to get in the way of Spiritual Truth. Help us to wrap our politics in love and compassion and then vote our own divinely guided conscience. Forgive us our errors as we forgive the errors of others. Help us to turn a deaf ear to those who would instill within us needless fear and cause us to attack one another. For if You are for us, what can ever work against us? May we rise above our petty conflicts and perceived differences so that this nation and this world will be elevated to its divine power and magnificence. We are blessed because we are the expressions of your love in action. May we live that Truth daily. In You we trust, for there is nothing else that will sustain us. We are eternally grateful.

Amen

Prayer for the Healing of the World

Dear God,

Help us to move beyond the illusions before us to see the Truth
that is always present.

Lift the fog from our minds and remove the erroneous belief that
we are separate from You.

Help us to remember ourselves as You created us, one with You
and each other.

Guide us and direct our feet that we may follow Your Divine Will
for our lives.

Take our hands away from their useless tasks, and teach us how to
lovingly touch the ones in darkness.

Remove the words from our mouths that hurt and destroy, and give
us new words of love that inspire and uplift.

Lead us to those places where we are most needed, and open our
hearts to the awareness of our gifts, that we might be a healing
light unto the world.

Thank You, God.

Amen

USE ME

Here I Am Lord; Use me—make of me an instrument of Your peace and loving kindness. Use all of me.

Take my heart, Lord—fill it with love so fully expressed that it may be a beacon to those seeking solace, comfort and rest.

Take my hands, Lord—give them the touch of healing love, so that new life is realized in all upon whom they are placed.

Take my eyes, Lord—fill them with only visions of Your Divine Perfection, that I may behold the Christ Presence within all humankind.

Take my ears, Lord—clear away the cacophony of earthly noises, that I may hear the music of the spheres and sing its song of love.

Take my mouth, Lord—fill it with words of inspiration, encouragement, love and praise, that all who hear my voice are transformed by the power of You in me.

Here I am, Lord—Use me—Use all of me

So that I AM your Will not mine, that the Divine purpose for which I came into this life is fulfilled, and that I may express the Divine Promise of Your love for all Your sons and daughters.

Here I AM Lord—Use me—Use all of me to the Glory of Thy Great Goodness.

I Will Pray for You

I Will Pray For You
When morning dawns within the hearts of all humanity
And the Robin's song connects the newborn day
For You, I Will Pray

I Will Pray For You
When the evening shade comes down upon the sky
And kisses the droopy eyelids of the sleepy day
For You, I will pray.

I Will Pray For You
When the autumn light casts shadows over the fallen leaves
And sparkling snowflakes light the wintry way.
For You, I Will Pray

I Will Pray For You
When the song of spring is heard in every place throughout the
earth
And the tulips shout that summer's on its way
For You, I Will Pray

I Will Pray For You
Tirelessly, unceasingly, that you are always in God's care,
Every second of every minute of each and every day
For You, My Friend . . . I Will Pray

36